first love

other books
by
ann kiemel anderson

Hi, I'm Ann

I'm Out to Change My World

I Love the Word Impossible

It's Incredible

Yes

I'm Celebrating

I'm Running to Win

I Gave God Time

Taste of Tears, Touch of God

Struggling for Wholeness

And with the Gift Came the Laughter

Open Adoption

God's Little Dreamer

ANN KIEMEL ANDERSON

Wolgemuth & Hyatt, Publishers, Inc.
Brentwood, Tennessee

The mission of Wolgemuth & Hyatt, Publishers, Inc. is to publish and distribute books that lead individuals toward:

- A personal faith in the one true God: Father, Son, and Holy Spirit;

- A lifestyle of practical discipleship; and

- A worldview that is consistent with the historic, Christian faith.

Moreover, the Company endeavors to accomplish this mission at a reasonable profit and in a manner which glorifies God and serves His Kingdom.

Published April 1991. First Edition.
Printed in the United States of America.
97 96 95 94 93 92 91 8 7 6 5 4 3 2 1

Unless otherwise noted, all Scripture quotations are from the New American Standard Bible, ©1960, 1962, 1963, 1968, 1971, 1972, 1973, 1975, 1977, by The Lockman Foundation and are used by permission.

Wolgemuth & Hyatt, Publishers, Inc.
1749 Mallory Lane, Suite 110
Brentwood, Tennessee 37027

Library of Congress Cataloging-in-Publication Data

Anderson, Ann Kiemel.
    First love / Ann Kiemel Anderson.
        p. cm.
    ISBN 1-56121-057-9
    1. Anderson, Ann Keimel. 2. Christian biography—United States.
3. Christian life—1960– I. Title.
BR1725.A33A3 1991
209'.2—dc20
    [B]   91-2157
                                                                       CIP

to
dr. henry brandt, my father-in-law,
and mike warnke, my hippie friend,
both of whom have drawn me back
to my First Love;

and

with special love to tiffany,
a part of our family;

and

paul and margaret pauley
who have replaced my parents.

I know your deeds and your toil
and perseverance . . .
you have perseverance and have
endured for My name's sake,
and have not grown weary.
But I have this against you,
that you have left your first love.

Revelation 2:2–4

contents

prologue:
whiter than snow

Lord Jesus,
I long to be perfectly whole.
I want Thee forever to live in my soul.
Break down every idol.
Cast out every foe.
Now wash me and I will be whiter than snow.

Lord Jesus,
I cling to Thy Throne in the sky.
Help me to make a complete sacrifice.
I give up myself,
and whatever I own.
Now wash me and I will be whiter than snow.

James Nicholson and William G. Fischer

acknowledgments

incredible respect and admiration for robert wolgemuth
and mike hyatt, the most patient publishers in the world.
giant human beings!

with special love to will and our sons, taylor, brock, colson,
and brandt. without them, there never would have been a
story.

introduction

will and i have been married nine years. we have lived to
mid-life. embarked on parenting in a big way.

both of us visionaries. strong-willed. spirited. dedicated.
committed to being good Christians, serving the Lord. at
least that is what we thought we were doing.

we started life and marriage and parenting with dreams,
huge gusto, and strength. from the world's perspective, we
appeared, i think . . . talented. basically pure. trying very
hard to earnestly be all we thought God wanted us to be.

will's father, in sincerity, taught will to "get the job done.
there is no excuse for man-failure." his dad was a brilliant,
accomplished man. he came to Jesus at the close of his life,
so will's modeling was limited. raised with tremendous integrity and courage, will still missed the truth of how pov-
erty-stricken he was without total dependence on God. no
matter how well he could get the job done.

my holy father truly understood his neediness of the Lord,
but he worked so hard at being perfect and good for God
that somewhere i ended up trying too hard, instead of trusting more.

we reached a point where we were like our mercedes with its blown engine. we looked good on the outside. underneath things weren't always working right. will and i found times when joy and peace and serenity and long-suffering were not obvious at all.

in this story, i allow you to journey with us as vulnerably as i know how.

somewhere along the way, among best intentions, good deeds, sincere hearts, we left our First Love. we started on course, and ever so subtly, we left the road. so gently that we did not even realize when we wandered off, or how far.

please stay with us through the trip. at moments, you will see us broken and beat up and stressed out. the amazing thing is that we felt that the stressful things were totally external to both of us. in fact, the stress we experienced was caused by our heart reaction to events around us.

when will and i would have conflict, we would promise ourselves not to let it happen again. we kept forgetting how "deceitfully and desperately wicked" the heart is. (jeremiah 17:9). we successfully deceived ourselves, over and over. "now that i know what to do, i'll do it." it was self-control at its best (or worst) instead of surrender to the Holy Spirit.

i found i could manage my behavior, but not my spirit. i drifted into actually believing that my self-controlled Christian acting was victorious living. at times i could scarcely handle the increased pressures brought my way, saying over and over, "i will try harder."

somewhere it became unintentional Christian acting. self-control versus surrender. i believed it was right.

we treasure our fathers' examples in many things. will and i now know that real peace comes from dealing with our hearts. a cleansed heart that relies on the Holy Spirit.

we are not just lovers in bed. we are learning to be friends. great friends. a team for the first time. together. still broken, crippled, weak and powerless except through the Holy Spirit's power. failing, and seeking His mercy and forgiveness, over and over.

never have i so struggled and toiled at something so simple as seeing my own sin. i was wrong. i am so sorry. forgive me. cleanse me. empower me. Jesus, please.

we share our story . . . our children's story . . . hoping some of you might find yourselves where we were . . . and will grab our hands and join us back on the path we originally, truly, desired to embrace. God's path. His trip. His glory. one that He must bring us back to again and again and again.

ann kiemel anderson
november, 1990

The cleansing stream . . .
I see . . . I see . . .
I plunge . . . and oh, it cleanseth
me . . . oh praise the Lord,
it cleanseth me. it cleanseth me.
It cleanseth me.

(Phoebbe Palmer Knapp)

1. *the red-checked umbrella*

brandt, our youngest, had been rocked and tucked into his little crib in the nursery. at nap and bedtime, i always crawl into the rocker . . . as i did with the others . . . and cradle my baby. sing all kinds of little songs over and over. kiss him. tell each one all the special things about him. his brown eyes or his blue eyes. his dark hair, or now, with colson, his blond, and taylor, his strawberry blond hair. his sturdy little legs. how i love his smile. the dimple in his cheek. and on and on. then with an earnest prayer, i nestle him under covers.

taylor, brock, and colson were waiting in the other bedroom, where they can all sleep together. crawling into the bottom double bunk, i pulled colson into my arms, with taylor and brock lying beside me.

"mommy, tell us about 'little billy goats gruff'," pleaded taylor.

"coco and bobo, mommy," colson asked, pulling on my face.

"mom," brock called . . .

"shhh, i am going to tell you one of my very favorite stories. tomorrow, daddy and i must fly to florida, and i want you to tuck this into your hearts."

everyone became very still, quiet.

"this is a story about a real lady. mommy once wrote about it, and they put it in a magazine.

"years ago, a little girl lived in africa with her dad and mom. her daddy was a missionary, sort of like my daddy was. it had not rained for three whole years.

"people were dying everywhere. and animals. everyone and everything needed water. one evening, frances courtney smith's father announced,

"'i am sending messages to all the outlying villages, informing them that tomorrow morning at ten, we are going to pray to our God . . . Jesus . . . for rain.'

"'papa, papa,' wailed frances courtney smith, 'you must not! if rain does not come, the natives will kill us . . . and it has not rained for three years!'

"'do not worry, darling,' papa answered. 'Jesus never fails.'

"that night, as frances courtney smith crawled into bed, she heard the drums in all the outlying villages, announcing to all that prayer would be given in the missionary's church. she shuddered, and buried her face into the pillow, pleading with God to do a miracle.

"early the next morning, she jumped out of bed and ran to the window. hoping, praying, there would be some clouds in the sky. the sun was scorching hot. every crack of earth was thirsty. no clouds. not even a hint. her little heart shuddered. as she looked toward the little church, she noticed people already gathering. pouring in from the jungles. filling the church. starting to line up outside, peeking in the windows.

"'oh, papa, i am SO afraid,' frances said.

"taking her hand, he led her over to the little church. frances walked down the aisle, and found a little spot on the front pew. her father, tall and strong, marched down the aisle. with warmth in his voice, he announced,

"'we have gathered today to pray to our Christian God for rain. let's pray . . . dear Lord, we are dying without rain. You have promised to meet all our needs. please send us rain. we trust You, Lord. amen.' he smiled at all who had gathered. many . . . most . . . did not know anything about Jesus, but had walked hours, desperate for a miracle from anywhere.

"frances courtney smith was horrified. why had not papa prayed a LONG prayer. with flowery words. pleading with God. God would NEVER hear that prayer!

"suddenly a little woman got off the bench next to her. she had cradled two babies, one under each arm, through the hot sun for several hours to get there. she did not know Jesus. she hesitated, and frances watched as she reached down to pick something else up. balancing each baby on her hips, she pulled out a little red-checked umbrella.

"frances courtney smith began to cry. she fell on her knees. though she was a little girl, she was amazed at this woman's faith. this little native mother really believed the missionary's God would answer prayer.

"'oh, Jesus,' wept frances, ' please give me that kind of faith . . . so i can grow up brave and strong for You.'"

my little sons were wide-eyed. utterly still. listening.

"later, at lunch, frances courtney smith said, 'oh, papa, do not be so happy. there is not a drop of rain anywhere. i am SO AFRAID we are going to die.'

"'oh, frances, i am not afraid. our God is good. i trust Him.'

"suddenly, frances hopped off the chair and ran to the window. she could scarcely believe her eyes. there was a cloud. not bigger than the size of her fist, but it was a cloud . . . and that was more than there had been in years.

"'papa . . . papa . . .' screamed frances, 'there is a cloud!'

"soon the sky was black, and rain was drenching the cracked earth. frances let it run down her face, her hair. she opened her mouth, and let it cool her hot tongue and throat.

"a miracle! a *real* miracle!

"frances kept thinking of that little native woman, baby tucked under each arm, and a red-checked umbrella opened over their heads.

"you ask me today what faith is? faith is a little, red-checked umbrella."

"mommy," brock spoke quietly, "is that REALLY a true story?"

"yes, darling," i began to softly cry. "isn't it beautiful? mommy has been so worried about getting her book done . . . and suddenly, i remember, too, that faith is as simple as a red-checked umbrella."

"mommy," taylor spoke. colson lying still in my arms.

"yes, taylor," i answered.

"i think i worry a lot."

"yes, darling. are you worried about something now?"

"uh-huh."

"are you worried about something happening to mommy and daddy when we fly to florida tomorrow?"

"uh-huh." his eyes were filled with tears.

it had been such a long day. we were to fly out at seven-thirty a.m. i had just placed another baby in a couple's arms. just watched the birth mother obey God, coura-geously, in her situation. i was exhausted. i *never* like leav-ing my children. there was still a lot to be done on this manuscript. without helping it, i began to cry, too.

"taylor, mommy loves you so. and brock and colson and brandt. you know . . . i already, today, felt Jesus reassuring me that it is all right. daddy and i will come home safely. Jesus whispered that to me today."

tucking the covers under their chins. kissing each little face one more time. reminding them to go right to sleep. that colson could go to HIS school (sunday school) the next day. he so wants to be like his big brothers.

being a mom. traveling with a husband. writing another book. loving, in a special way, pregnant girls . . . and run-ning beside them. trying to be Jesus where i am.

sometimes, the days are so long. the moments intense. the demands extraordinary. i will never be enough. i remind my children of that every day. only Jesus is enough. and faith like a red-checked umbrella.

2. *stress*

the most painful year of my life was 1989. everything . . .
and i mean every word . . . i had ever written or spoken of
hope and peace and promise and God's love and assurance
of sunrises had to be stretched and tested and tried to the
ninth degree.

we were invited on a glorious vacation in the caribbean
with some of our favorite, favorite people. i could taste the
warm sun and virgin piña coladas in the sand by the sparkling atlantic. it was february, 1989, and i had four beautiful, cherished little sons, four-and-a-half and under. the
baby was just four months old, and this was the first time i
had left him. no middle of the night disturbance. no little
hands to wash over and over. or little bottoms to wipe, or
multiple diapers to change. or meals to cook or laundry.

i loved every bit of motherhood and the care of my small
sons. i really did. but a romantic trip with my husband,
and a week with loving adults sounded perfect.

after a long trip to miami, we all connected in great excitement and united in an exotic resort, in a rather palatial
house with our own housekeeper.

the first major disappointment came when everyone else's
bags arrived, but not ours. my swimsuits, my sandals, my
shorts and teeshirts . . . and all my dressy evening wear
was nowhere to be found. i am so much more petite than

the other three women, so i was mainly stuck with what i
had on. something i had donned in idaho in sub-zero
weather. warm clothes and miserable shoes.

though this resort was elite, it did not have shopping centers and shoe stores. the normal amenities in our kind of situation. one of the men was larger than will, but had sharp
things that he could wear. along with clean underwear and
socks.

i know we are to "rejoice always." i know i took it harder
than normal. i was very tired and spent, and my exhilara-
tion was so high that such a jolt just kind of knocked me
off my feet.

will did have a toothbrush. we could share. and the
women pulled out things they could help me with. my feet
blistered in my winter pumps, and i so wanted to feel
pretty and glamorous each night when we all dressed up,
and visited a new, elegant restaurant.

for four days, my friend and i took the golf cart to the little
airport . . . on the back roads . . . to see if our luggage had
been located. to me, four days seemed like an eternity! will
was so resilient and happy. and handled it much better
than i.

i had had an ear infection (with small children, i have
picked up so many more bugs), and been on potent antibiotics for two weeks previous to our trip. the medicine in
my system made my skin allergic to the sun. and the one
thing i most loved to do . . . lie in the sun and read and
tan, i began to find difficult. my skin would itch and
scream unbelievably until i crawled into the shade. though
i tanned quickly, and did get some sun, the sacrifice i made

for it pretty much stole the joy and excitement. one other wife and i loved the sun. everyone else was an avid golfer, including will.

always, i had promised myself i would never be like some mothers i know who took a vacation, and moped for their children the entire trip. i wanted to be brave. mature. relaxed. i so wanted to enjoy my rest while i could. and solitude with my husband. i was very careful not to speak too much about the children (everyone else in the group had grown children).

by the sixth day, however, i longed for a glimpse of my children. all really babies. i had not been homesick since i was a child, and had forgotten the ache around one's heart . . . the longing in the pit of my stomach. the thought, "would i ever see them again? kiss their faces? cuddle them? laugh with them? feel the grasp of their small hands in mine?" i had not remembered how much homesickness can hurt.

we loved our friends very much. we had beautiful dinners in serene, balmy, elegant little places around the island. we laughed together and cried together and shared on a deep level.

i did not feel really good about myself. my shoes and one warm dress did not make it very exotic.

i returned home with some sad feelings. (they did locate our bags a couple of days before we left!)

a few weeks later, i began feeling sick. nauseated. some abdominal cramping. no period for three months. a couple of

times, i had taken a pregnancy test, and was sad each time
to discover a negative response.

pregnancy tests represent the most seizing, powerful memories of my life. all the times my hopes soared, to discover
negative results and only a late period. all the times the results were positive, but only lasted for a few weeks or
months before i miscarried. i have already written plenty
on my infertility in other books, but suffice it to say that no
words can adequately articulate the pain an infertile
woman endures . . . and i really had resolved to not subject
myself to that pain again.

i did continue to have abdominal pain, and no period. finally, my family doctor sent me for a lower g.i. something i
had never experienced before. drinking pretty foul (to me)
stuff the night before. going to the bathroom all night. preparing for them to pump you with fluids to x-ray your in-
testinal tract. i had heard horror stories about this particular test. all the fluid running out before they could x-ray.
nausea. and other unpleasant things. i took my clothes off
and donned the generic gown and robe they give everyone.
mine was at least four sizes too big for me, and i clung to
the gaping opening as i sat beside other women on the
couch waiting my turn.

the technician asked me to take my robe off and crawl onto
the cold, hard table. she positioned the covers above my abdomen and walked back behind the door to snap the x-ray.

suddenly, she peaked out, asking, "you're not pregnant,
right?"

"right," i responded assuredly.

"when was your last period?" her next question.

"well . . . three months ago . . . but i am POSITIVE i am not pregnant because i have had two negative pregnancy tests!" she walked over to me, looking shocked. "three months since a period?"

"yes, but PLEASE take this test, and get it over with. I really am POSITIVE."

"ann, i cannot do this abdominal x-raying without a pregnancy test. it could seriously damage a baby!" the technician looked alarmed.

"PLEASE," i exclaimed. "just let me call my doctor and he can reassure you."

"okay . . . the phone is over on the wall."

"julian," i panicked, "they do not want to do a lower g.i. without a pregnancy test. will you just let me put the technician on the line so you can tell her to go ahead?"

"ann," my doctor hesitated, "i think it would not hurt to take one more pregnancy test just for precaution."

"oh, julian," i wailed.

i could not imagine feeling this sick, and living through that g.i. prep again.

exasperated, i pulled on the prison-striped robe, grabbed the pink slip, and headed toward the lab. refusing to get dressed, and demanding fast reporting so i could get through the g.i. without losing everything they had put into me, i roamed the halls, in robe, looking for the sign "laboratory."

i delivered some urine, and walked back to radiology, waiting to be called.

suddenly a nurse appeared, and said, "ann, your doctor wants to speak with you. the phone is against that wall," she pointed.

"ann," julian responded solemnly, "your pregnancy test is very positive."

i cannot remember EVER being so stunned.

"julian, i do not believe it. i don't. call the lab again. tell the lady she must have made an error, and to check it again."

refusing to walk away without getting this g.i. test, i waited for julian to call back.

"ann," announced julian, "the lady in the lab use to work for me. she is very proficient. she is not likely to make a mistake, and she said the test registered positive immediately!"

i stumbled back to the little cubby hole to put my clothes on. wonder. terror. shock. dismay. and slowly, a quiet joy that this must really be a miracle, and so, surely, this pregnancy would survive!

slowly, i absorbed the reality, and will and the children were ecstatic. another baby in the family. maybe a little girl. never could we love one from our own flesh even a hair more than taylor, brock, colson, and brandt. but the idea of a healthy pregnancy was thrilling. something i longed to experience since childhood. the dream had utterly died for Jesus to make it live. i always felt, deep in my heart, that this particular life experience would come about.

we took the four little boys camping with bob and sheila and amy, their daughter. also, a birthmother and birthfather, three weeks from delivery, joined us.

i had NEVER taken an official camping trip. tents. cooking over an open fire. using public bathrooms. three of my four children were still in diapers, and i was leery.

bob and sheila were such great friends, though. and pros at camping. they brought all the food and they and will cooked it. and we all shared in the cost. they attached mountain bikes for us to ride, and we located by a naturally warm, hot-springs pool that was unforgettable. we did not have to take showers in the rather dirty, public bath . . . only to swim in the pool of natural hot springs that was hot like a bath, and drained every night to put all fresh water in every morning thereafter.

being pregnant, i was the only one to have a cot in a tent, and i did have excuses to feel tired and lazy.

brandt and colson were still not walking, and in a double stroller. will took taylor and brock fishing daily . . . hiking . . . digging worms. they loved it, and the babies slept through every night.

i still find it hard to believe that people find it exhilarating to sleep in a tent with no bathroom close-by. no matter how many times i would walk over to the public bath-

room, every night, all night, i had to go . . . just knowing
there was no place to do it.

everyone else slept well. i got up and down all night, every
night. being a mother, though, there is nothing i can think i
might not do . . . if wholesome and fun . . . to watch my little boys and their daddy clap their hands. share stories by
the fire. giggle in sleeping bags in the tent, thrilled for
mommy and daddy to be right there with them. motherhood tends to strip away much of my rigidity. to stretch
the love from one child's bold, small heart to the next one's.

bob and sheila were fun. giving. they fried eggs and bacon
and pancakes in the morning, and created wonderful dinners at night. the thought of life growing in me always
gave me a serene-yet-exhilarated peace and joy.

the next week, will sent me to a specialist in california. i
had no bleeding, but a lot of abdominal pain . . . and my
success with pregnancy was zero. visiting a specialist
seemed logical.

always loving the word "impossible" in a very unique
way, i completely embraced, with faith, the life of this
baby. i refused to reflect back to all the failures, previously,
that left painful wounds.

in california, the doctor ran all kinds of tests. he discovered
that i had an extremely strong adrenal gland. that i was
very healthy overall. but very depleted from the years of infection and miscarriage and surgeries, all pregnancy-re-
lated. he also proved something that i basically knew already . . . i had an unbelievable resistance to ANY
medication. where most people respond either extremely
well to medicine, or even normally with some relief, my

urine showed that i absorbed almost none of it in my system.

sending me to a downstairs office to have more blood-work done, he first gave me some medication, and asked me to take a certain amount that day and evening so they could check my urine again. before i left, one of the nurses called out,

"ann, i just want you to know we did a pregnancy test on you to check blood levels, and it appears to be negative. the doctor is extremely surprised, and wants to do a better one in the morning."

i was checked into a hotel a few miles away. a brand new, very classy hilton, and i crawled out of the office in such terror and shock i could scarcely breathe.

the pregnancy test negative? how could that be. God could not . . . would not . . . play such a horribly nasty, dirty trick on me. it was the all-time, darkest, most terrifying moment of my entire life. the most humiliating. the most shattering. the one moment i prayed i would never live to see. that my hope could be so utterly dashed that i did not know if i could ever believe in God again.

if my proven, long-time friend, rosemary, had not been there, i am not sure how i could have survived. it was that awful.

alone, in that beautiful hotel room . . . away from will and my little boys and parents and friends . . . i literally fought for my life.

my established, long-tested relationship with the Savior
was shaking so out of control that i feared i would experience an actual breakdown. feared that i COULD lose all my
faith which had always been extremely resilient and tough.

desperately, i called jan, my sister, in cleveland. there was
no way she . . . or maybe anyone . . . in that moment could
console me. God had to physically grasp ahold of my shoul-
ders and reach down and grip my heart and hold me with
all His strength until i could see the morning light. until i
knew that i knew that i knew Jesus was good. He did care
and love. He would keep me at least swaying on my ut-
terly-stricken and trembling legs of faith.

i could not sleep. my heart raged with grief. i literally
clung to the bed, sobbing.

"Jesus, WHY? i never asked to get pregnant again. i did
not feel i could live through another loss. not another one."

who did God think i was? did He assume my heart was
cast in steel?

somehow, before morning, i had . . . somehow . . . by Jesus'
grace . . . decided i would follow Jesus forever, and though
i felt kicked in the stomach, i had come too far with Him to
let go. to detach from Jesus would have been as serious to
my well-being as literally cutting my heart out, and leaving
a gaping, groaning wound.

morning dawned. in the first moments of light, i realized
this prison experience could not possibly compare to any
other pain in my entire life. my emotions and soul were
still behind revolting bars, but they were alive, and they

would push my spirit into a new me, generous and wide
. . . into freedom and someday joy.

pulling on my clothes, i had rosemary (one of the dearest
people in the entire world to me) drive me to the medical
clinic. i still could not believe i had somehow miscarried.
the thought of another pregnancy that failed chilled my
bones.

hardly able to walk with my head ringing so wildly, i gave
a sample of urine and they tested it.

"incredible, ann," mused the doctor. "i can scarcely find
one trace of medication in your urine. you are at the top
one percent in the world who don't absorb medicine."

another pregnancy test revealed another negative report,
and they assumed i was too depleted to carry it, and the
sac had absorbed right into the uterine wall.

two days later when rosemary dropped me at the airport,
my heart was still crushed, but not flattened to an irrevers-
ible place. i longed to see will and the children. to see jan
soon. to let go, *forever*, the dream of a healthy pregnancy in
my body.

three days later, home again, basking in the glow of my
family's heart (i WAS the most blessed woman on earth . . .
i *had* to be . . . my gifts were displayed everywhere i
looked).

i had been in prison, and released . . . but not for long.
three days later, at home, i suddenly bent over with the
most excruciating pain. i could not walk, and i could

scarcely breathe. the right side of my abdomen throbbed, but my appendix had been removed years ago in college.

getting someone to come to the house with the children, will rushed me to family emergency. were my children going to grow up thinking we lived, partially, in the emergency room?

brock said, "mommy, is the emergency room you are going to tonight that other one with the playroom?"

i sobbed in humiliated desperation. they had defined each emergency room with a unique trait that made it bearable for them.

"yes, darling, and i will be right back i am sure."

the hospital had seen me through a lot of emergencies, and could see when i displayed that kind of pain that i was sick. very sick. they immediately inserted an i.v. and gave me some pain medication so they could calm me down enough to examine me.

a wonderful physician, rocco, started checking me. he felt my right abdominal cavity was swollen. they admitted me to the hospital and i cried more over being admitted than even the pain. i have to be REALLY ill to allow them to keep me at a hospital.

the next morning, jim, my ob-gyn, put me in surgery to just peek into my abdomen and see what there might be. it revealed a serious abscess in my right ovary and tube. either a result of the miscarriage, or the abscess was responsible for the lost baby.

for ten days, i lay flat in bed, with an i.v. of the most potent antibiotic surging through my system. to control the
pain so i would not get off the bed and literally crawl
around the floor, groaning, they ordered me a morphine
shot every three to four hours. because i am so resistant,
they had to inject something potent. for hours, though, i
would sense little relief.

my fever rose. my infection persisted. the potent antibiotic
did not faze the abscess.

on the eleventh day, away from will and the children, and
totally depressed, they wheeled me into surgery, and did a
major operation to remove the right ovary and tubes.

it would have been hard on anyone's system, but after all
my miscarriages and infections and just losing another
pregnancy, my body was more spent and crushed (as was
my spirit) than ever.

being a marathon runner . . . running eight 26.2-mile dis-
tances . . . i had always prided myself on the tough resilient endurance and strength i possessed. now i felt i had
completely lost my health and would never regain it.

with our beautiful little boys, barely five and under, i
feared i would *NEVER* be whole again. never even be
strong enough to help raise them.

two days out of the hospital, i began to feel violently sick.
it was late july. stifling hot. i limped out to the little wad-
ing pool and soaked with the little boys.

i began to feel something never before experienced come over me. i could not define it. i failed in easing the wild, tearing force in my body.

a doctor from the south called. he had received my private phone number from a close personal friend. he could not get me out of his mind. he had read some of my books.

"i think i am cracking up," i pushed each word out with panic. "i am scared. really scared. am i going to die?"

the doctor asked what medications they had given me.

"intravenous antibiotics, and lots of them for ten days . . . but it never helped . . . i just do not think it is related to that," i cried.

"ann, what did they give you for pain?"

"pain?" i felt shocked. what did that have to do with anything?

"they gave me several things, but before the surgery, they gave me a shot of morphine every three hours to keep me still. after the surgery, oral pain medicine and antibiotics. the shots though, lasted through about ten days, pre-op."

"ann, i volunteer some nights at a drug rehabilitation center, and i bet you are addicted to morphine!"

"addicted?" i started sobbing. "what do you mean 'addicted'?"

"ann, do not be angry with the hospital. sometimes, patients are so sick they naturally develop addictions because they have to have so much medication for recovery and healing."

addiction.

that is the awful word that only other people experience. high-powered businessmen behind classy, polished doors, sniffing cocaine. the down and out, lying on sidewalks and park benches. not me. that was impossible!

"Jesus, i am screaming at You. please, Jesus, save me. i am drowning. the cliff is trembling as i cling to the edge of the rock."

"what do i do?"

"call your internist, ann, and tell him what you think. have him call me. will must physically get you out of the house to a quiet, dark place. morphine is physiological. cocaine is psychological. i believe, ann, the morphine is harder to come off of."

will checked me into a lovely hotel in idaho falls.

while will worked all day, i battled withdrawal in the dark hotel room. i crawled around. tried to sleep. soaked in hot tubs of water, trying to cleanse my body of the unforgettably horrible sensation inside.

will came every evening for dinner, and spent the night. amy and tiffany, and some other beautiful friends, came in and took care of my children until the morphine was out of my system. my lovely mother-in-law, jo, flew in from florida to help.

no wonder thousands of people do not walk away from drugs. no wonder their courage is watery and weak. so many do not feel they have anything to fight so hard for.

because it is hard. it is brutal. it takes the guts and determination of a marathon runner to grow beyond it.

before one makes blanket, pious statements about drugs, be kind and allow the Holy Spirit to show one's own sinfulness.

we *must* walk in each other's shoes to genuinely know the pain. the devastation.

it took me five days of hell to pull my system through it. there is some pain you forget. this pain i will never lose touch with.

i returned home from the hotel, weak but free of morphine in my system.

i am revolted by morphine. my little boys were so lonely for me. they love their daddy, but a mom to a little boy is unique. his very own confidante and representative. the one who tends to see the purest and best in him.

all the days of battling the abscess left my abdomen full of adhesions and throbbing. even after the ovarial tubes were removed. the ordeal of withdrawing from the morphine left my body so weak that i could only stand . . . or sit up . . . for very short hours.

never will i hold the doctors accountable for the morphine experience. i was agonizingly sick, and with my tremendous resistance to medication, they had to use something very potent to keep me quiet, and close to a prone position.

the drug battle was one of the most powerful experiences of my life. always, i had shaken my head at drug users. wagged my mental finger at them. exclaimed the atrocities. intellectualized the deliverance.

but . . . until one has been there . . . until one has actually tasted withdrawal . . . one cannot lovingly, and with empathy, truly judge.

i had a terrific husband. four beautiful, fine sons. a life with mission and purpose. i had a giant God at work in and for me. there was a lot for me to fight for. many have no support on front lines, or any taste of goodness to stay in battle for.

the human spirit is an amazing thing. with incredible strength and courage. even though the morphine experience was nothing i could control . . . nothing i knowingly embraced, once my body was addicted to it, i moved into the arena where all drug-users exist: a craving for ANYTHING to quickly take away the nightmare one's body is feeling.

after the five days of battle, clean but completely spent, i went home to my little family, and basked in their love.

two days later, our house sold. after a year . . . totally unprepared . . . we had one month to move. the whole family was excited, but me.

"honey, you will have to do everything. i'm just not up to it."

"don't worry, sweetheart. it will be a piece of cake. a few friends from the church and a u-haul one day will have us in in no time. relax."

will organized the move the last week with one trip every night in a pickup . . . our lovely church friends giving up a saturday to get big items in the u-haul for three trips. and we were really in. i thought it was just what i needed to direct my attention off myself.

i learned later that each move can cost you a year of saturdays . . . getting settled in. getting unpacked . . . giving the home your own touch . . . this was our first move. i had so much to learn!

3. our birthmothers

i write this from my heart. i share our story. please know it
does not mean i feel the entire world should live just like
us. most everything is negotiable, i think . . . the only absolute is embracing Jesus. every person, every race, every
color, everywhere. every moment. everyday.

our third son, colson, was born when taylor was three-and-
a-half and brock was two-and-a-half. we had prayed daily
. . . all of us . . . for another baby. though we had been of-
fered several, we could not seem to feel peace.

colson's birthmother came to idaho. will and i had flown to
her home town to meet her and her family. three days
later, she flew home with us. will headed for africa on business. colson was born almost three weeks later, a little
earlier than expected, and will had to find the quickest
flight home. susan and i and dr. oldroyd survived delivery
together. it was my hardest delivery experience because
susan became toxic, but she was very brave and beautiful
and strong.

we fell in love with susan's family. vibrant believers . . .
clear to colson's eighty-seven year old great grandmother.
my friend, amy, said to me by phone, "oh, ann, you and
will have a wonderful baby. he (we knew ahead it was a
boy by ultrasound) comes from the most wonderful
family!"

don and donna (susan's parents) are warm and strong and bonded to us for life. sisters, brother, aunts, uncle. it was and has been, truly, a family affair.

many special women each did a beautiful patch for a personal patchwork quilt that we will cherish forever, and share with colson.

named after our dear friends, chuck colson and raymond berry, colson was placed in our arms by our special, loved birthmother. we were heading for the greatest adventure of our lives!

i took susan and her mother to jackson, wyoming, for a day before they left. her mom had stayed with me until susan was released from the hospital. she has become one of my best friends and susan, my child.

i had to muster great courage at moments. a three-and-a-half year old and a two-and-a-half year old. will in africa. i, exhausted from all the long hours of labor and delivery. the incredible excitement. terrified that i could never measure up to susan and her mom.

but Jesus has NEVER asked us to do anything beyond the grace He covered us with to accomplish it.

the morning susan was to go to court to sign the final papers, i called her.

"susan, you remember you are not in a corner you cannot get out of. you can still take colson home with you. i will get him all ready for the plane."

each time i have done that, my heart silently shakes. but i have always loved my birthmothers more . . . and wanted God's will for their lives more . . . than i have wanted the miraculous, lovely, new little life that i already had snuggled under my heart.

"i know, ann," susan replied.

about an hour later, there was a knock on my door. when i opened it, i found susan and her mom.

"what happened?" i quietly, gently asked.

"i did it!" susan responded. a twinkle and some tears in her eyes.

"you did it? you really did it? we get to watch him grow up?" i asked, tears swimming in my eyes.

"yes, it is done."

i threw my arms around susan, crying and kissing her. then around donna.

oh! colson had truly become my little son! the joy covered every wall. every corner. every patch of space in the house.

taylor and brock had been so mellow. easy-going. serene as babies. colson was not!

he awakened every two hours screaming for a bottle. from the earliest days, he wanted me, and only me. when i left him at yolanda's (my terrific babysitter's), she would put a tape of me addressing some audience into the recorder so he thought i was somewhere close. pretty clever. it worked.

colson was the most intimate baby i have had. he snuggled. he nestled his little head right up under my arm as close to me as he could get. he would relax his beautiful, little body into any curve of me he could find.

have you ever tried writing a book with four little boys around you? it is now six o'clock in the morning. the house quiet. the world dark. i am scrunched up in bed, tablet in arm, and beside and around me are three of my four sons. both the two year olds.

"mommy!"

"shhhh!"

"mommy! mommy! what ya doin', mom?"

"colson, i am writing a book. QUIET!"

will has long gone to the office. (sigh.)

when colson was about six months old, we all (taylor and brock, too) boarded a plane to see susan and all the family. there was going to be a big evening, sponsored by the pregnancy crisis center where susan had first heard of my book, *Open Adoption.*

their church . . . very large . . . was packed. warm music and then lucy introduced susan. beautiful, dark-eyed eighteen year old girl. for the first time in her life, she boldly walked onto the platform and stood behind a microphone. with courage and poise, she shared her story of getting pregnant. of compromising. of feeling her life had come to an end. of being given my book . . . and saying, "this is the family for my baby."

following her moving, miraculous story, susan introduced me. before speaking, will and all three little boys (colson in his arms) came "on stage". there we stood, in a line, will holding one of susan's hands, and my arm around her shoulder. the handsome birthfather, truly sweet, was in the audience. quietly covered by the crowd.

later, when colson was a little over a year, i left him and brock with susan and her parents while i flew on to speak. brock slept with susan every night. donna rocked colson. what fun they had! and i had fun, too. five days of a break from little boys pulling on my skirt. changing diapers.

when colson was six months old, our fourth extraordinary birth mother flew to idaho. twenty-two. she had read my books and stood in autograph lines since she was ten. another boy, the ultrasound said! we were thrilled. what buddies they could be.

two months before sarah arrived, i met her and my other three birthmothers in a hotel for two days. i had to speak one of the nights, and it seemed a fun idea to bring them all in together. for my first three to meet sarah, and sarah them.

i had rooms side-by-side. a video of the little boys for them to watch. good food. hours of sharing about the children. about where the girls are in their journeys. time to prepare sarah for what was ahead. to ooh over beautiful baby clothes she had bought for the baby . . . and matching outfits for him and colson.

my dear friend, debby, lined up four of the sharpest Christian guys she could find for my birthmothers. i wanted them to have fun. to have a neat date.

"ann, we are not going without you!" they announced.

"oh, of course you are! will's not here, and i would be a tag-along."

"no, ann, we want YOU! we don't want to be cheated out of ANY time with you." they begged.

they are all so very pretty. in many ways, so much alike. so young and fresh and vibrant. how could i EVER be good enough for my little boys? would my little sons, if they knew them, think i was old and unglamorous and blah next to them?

a great dinner. four birthmothers, even eight months pregnant sarah, each with a very neat guy. a doctor. a psychologist. a college student and a businessman.

afterwards, i was to keynote a large, outdoor affair of several thousand. they were all in the audience. what i had not told them was that the children, who were down the freeway in another hotel, would be introduced. at the close of my speech, i announced my children (then only three . . . brandt still unborn).

donna, colson's grandmother, led them all out to me. beautifully dressed in smocked outfits. new little saddle shoes. colson, four months old. though they were far away, and just little figures on the stage, liz and karen could see taylor and brock (three-and-a-half and two-and-a-half) . . . it was the first time since they were babies. the crowd cheered. applauded.

"i would also like all of you to know," i spoke, "that my birthmothers are in the audience tonight, sitting around you. our fourth birthmother is also here, due to deliver our fourth little son in six weeks."

the crowd seemed awestruck. overwhelmed. they cheered.

the next day, as we were preparing to go our separate ways, the thought of liz and karen not really seeing taylor and brock haunted me. i know there are boundaries. lines to be drawn. at least, *we* all feel that way. but i wondered if the little boys would really understand, and could the girls have one more closer peak at them. their speech. their expressions. their spirits.

"liz and karen, i have an idea. why don't we go to the hotel where the boys are. you sit in the lobby, and i will go up and get taylor and brock for a walk. you can watch us walk by you . . . and follow behind aways, and enjoy just a piece of them."

"REALLY?" they exclaimed. "oh, ann, could we? oh that would be SO GREAT! so special!"

i got the little boys, fresh and sparkling, and came down the elevator. holding hands, we walked through the lobby, past the girls, to the front doors. just as i started to push them open (the children speaking rapidly because they were so thrilled to be with me) that Still Small Voice . . . the One most of us are too busy to listen to or even know . . . seemed to say,

"ann, let liz and karen see the boys one more time. it is okay."

through the years, in trial and error, i have tried not to second guess the Voice. only to obey it. instantly . . .

"taylor . . . brock . . . would you love to meet two of mommy's favorite friends in the whole world?"

"uh-huh," they smiled. so fresh-faced. so innocent. so utterly vulnerable and trusting.

walking over to shocked liz and karen, i announced,

"liz and karen, i would like you to meet my two sons, taylor and brock."

they instantly took their hands. smiled radiantly.

"do you want to go look for bugs with my mom and me?" brock asked.

we all took a little walk. held hands. the girls got close to their small faces. quietly spoke and shared with them about the leaves. the pool. felt their small, priceless hands . . . fingers . . . wrapped around their own.

when we returned to the hotel, i said, "taylor and brock, mommy must go do some things. can you hug and kiss my friends . . . and squeeze them tightly . . . before i take you up to your room?"

they kissed and hugged necks. i delivered the children back to the hotel room. kisses and kisses, and tight hugs and squeezing of colson. and i left and found liz and karen outside the door, weeping.

throwing their arms around my neck, they wept. and i did.

"oh, ann, we will never forget you did this. never. thank you so much for allowing those priceless moments, etched in our minds forever."

some would not understand. would question. but i heard God's voice. i know i did. the moment was as thrilling and rewarding for me as it was for them, and my little boys never picked up on anything.

how hard it was to wave good-bye to my birthmothers. sarah would be coming to idaho in two or three weeks. the others would be going back to their arenas. i was again letting go of some of my children. that is how i felt. the encounter was a memory etched in our hearts for life.

seeing again that brock laughed just like his mom. that taylor had the same quiet, humble spirit as liz. that colson had the white blond hair and blue eyes of his father, but the beautiful, olive skin of his mother. the exactly-same shape of her feet.

ice cream and snacks. laughing over the video. sometimes crying. learning of my birthmothers' spiritual journeys. romances. longings and desires. they are so much a part of the very essence of who i am, for they are flesh and blood of my sons whom i cherish and love far more than life itself.

as the children grow, i will ALWAYS stay in touch with their birthmothers. always love them as part of me. celebrate every victory. fiercely pray and believe for each trial. the little boys will not know until they are grown.

*Jesus, thank You for the beauty and majesty of Your place. Your
ways are so much better than ours. You be glorified, glorified,
glorified.*

we received this from chuck colson:

March, 1989

Dear Colson,

Welcome to the world.

I am very honored to learn that you have been named after me.
I'm going to take a very special interest in you. For one thing, I
will be praying for you regularly.

In her letter telling me of your arrival, your mother told me that
she and your dad hoped you would emulate me. More important than emulating me is to emulate the One whom I follow,
Jesus Christ, God's only Son.

My prayer for you, Colson, is that you will follow much earlier
than I did, at forty years.

Jesus is real. The very most important thing in your life will be
to come to know Him well, and be obedient to Him. Nothing
else in life matters.

I love your mom and dad very much.

                                        I love you.
                                        Chuck Colson

colson's birthmom and birthgrandparents came for thanksgiving weekend, 1990. colson was two and a half. one more
time to peek in on his spirit, and ours—.

Dear Ann,

I'm sitting here tonight, captivated with memories I have stored
deep in my heart. I think about the last four years I have spent
with my newfound family. How I feel I've known you all my
life, realizing its only been two years and nine months. I will
never forget the night I sat up and read your book, *And with the
Gift Came Laughter*, beginning to end. In awe that open adoption
was possible. How could it be true? I was an eighteen year old
girl, seven-and-a-half months pregnant, scared and almost out of
hope when you, Will, and God came to my rescue. There was
light put back in my life. Hope that God heard my deepest
plea. . . .

I came to Idaho after knowing you for two days. I wasn't about
to question God. I had prayed and prayed that He would find a
family that would not take my baby and hide. People told me I
was crazy. "You just can't do adoption and have it the way you
want it, Susan," they would say. "You are wasting your time trying to find anyone that would let you keep contact." How sad I
was that these people of God had such little faith. I've never
been happier that I didn't give in. It was hard standing alone,
but I guess I wasn't alone with God. Anyway, I knew what I was
doing with you and Will was right. I knew that Colson would be
better off with a solid family. I knew I could love Colson and we
could probably make it—but he would miss out on the most
wonderful part of life, so I believe. Two strong people, committed to one another for life and to God. The unconditional love I
know from my parents. I had that growing up, and I wanted
NOTHING less for my very own flesh! Ann, you have taught me
many great lessons. The very most important one is faith in God.
I have never met two more committed people—EVER. Nothing

in life means more to me than Colson. I love him unconditionally. I never knew what that kind of love meant until he came along. Watching you guys with all four boys leaves me in awe. You guys love each of them so strongly. You give each of them the secureness of your love. You are so dear to them. I can't even begin to tell you how that makes me feel.

I sit here tonight filled with emotion. Remembering tonight, laying with Colson. Asking him about the love he has for his Mommy and Daddy. He turned to me and said "I love my Mommy and Daddy, and Taylor and Brock and Brandt." He smiled from ear to ear. His eyes were beaming. I praise God for you and Will never questioning who I was. . . .

I trust you completely with Colson. I couldn't have done a better job myself. You were God's plan for Colson and me. I pray for you always! I pray specifically for you, Will, Taylor, Brock, Colson and Brandt, that you guys will be happy and live full lives under God! Thank you for being only you. . . . I thank you for having me and my family out for Thanksgiving! Thank you for letting me be a part of your family. . . . I will miss you when I go back home. If only our times together never had to end. . . .

All my love,

Susan

4. *fourth son*

sarah arrived in idaho falls, radiant, a few weeks before her due date. she stayed with bob and sheila, some of our dearest friends.

with colson, my third, it took me a few weeks, of feeling very topsy-turvy, disjointed, disorganized, left-footed before i began to fall into a rhythm.

now we were preparing for our fourth, and i absolutely felt ready. taylor and brock had each other to play with . . . and they adored and loved colson almost to his distraction and constant irritation. they were ALWAYS wanting to hold him, to get him to smile. to coo.

another baby would not be hard. colson was just crawling around. the new one would sleep a lot so i could give each of them plenty of focused attention. it certainly sounds good, doesn't it. i KNEW the fourth would be mellow. he would have to be with three others.

we all had such fun with sarah. she journalized. read. played with us. we had hours to share. her baby was going to be the sibling to the other three, and she got to see how we really lived. the boys adored her.

most people thought we were crazy, i assume. as i look back on it, i believe it was a miracle that will felt good about it. he made the final decisions, so i know brandt was truly to be ours.

sarah had struggled with her decision. the birthfather (whom we had met) was handsome, warm, charming. he had liberal means to provide for them. it was sarah's decision, and once she made it, there was no ambivalence.

rocco, one of my favorite people in the world, delivered brandt. will and i were there. another time, i watched this utterly beautiful girl, warm-spirited and gentle, bravely . . . so bravely . . . labor and deliver one of my sons.

everyone needs to be in on a labor-delivery experience a few times. only then, can one know the depth of love . . . and courage it takes to bring a child into the world. after having the privilege of assisting girls many, many times in the delivery room, i hold the experience in sacred awe. with deep, quiet respect.

will's sister, chrisi, was here and out in the waiting room, as were sheila, her daughter, amy, and many others. i cannot remember sarah even murmuring when she pushed brandt out. great celebration exploded in the room. sarah and i began to weep. i kissed her and kissed her. (i cried and felt utter awe at ALL my son's births, and the love for these brave girls was boundless).

brandt was rosy and plump. eight pounds, nine ounces. lots of black hair. a quiet, serene baby. colson was born february 11, will's birthday month. brandt was born september 1, my birthday month. labor day week-end. Sarah had bought an exquisite, blue-lace dress and gorgeous blanket for him to go home in. her beautiful mother and her mother's lovely friend came to be with her. they flew home the day after she was released, and again, my heart was punctured and shaken. to know her pain and loss. to feel my ecstasy and sadness, both. to look into the face of this perfect, flawless baby, and know he was really mine. i had FOUR sons. it still brings tears to my eyes.

> beauty for ashes.
> from seeming ruin to glory.
> from a sense of rebellion (normal) to
> true obedience and submission.
> with many tears, but love rooted so
> deep in the soil of my heart that
> it could never be shaken.

brandt is named william brandt, after his daddy and his grandpa, dr. henry brandt.

all four were circumcised on the eighth day, and will and i and each child preceding the baby witnessed it. taylor, brock, colson watched after will's prayer, in reverent curiosity. for brandt, even six-month-old-colson, with his big brothers, attended. we are a family. that is a family affair.

when sarah flew home, will and i left the three older ones, and took brandt to sun valley with dear friends, john and anna, for the weekend. we felt this little one needed focused attention. some time that was his very own with us, and i was so exhausted after the emotional and intense labor and delivery . . . and telling dear sarah good-bye.

four little sons. three-and-a-half, two-and-a-half, six months and newborn. big, sprawling house. fan mail. writing assignments. appearances. i did it all myself, except for a

very wonderful cleaning lady coming on fridays, and a
great secretary in my office downtown.

have you ever traveled with four tiny boys? the entire
plane disrupts when we board. passengers gape in a mix of
horror and awe and delight. no one wants to sit close to
you. you check into a hotel room. two cribs. a king-sized
bed. babies crying. the bigger boys chasing each other. as
we get ready to go out the door for me to speak, the baby
regurgitates all over my silk suit. my hair. all over him.

i said to will once, "honey, i am going to take a quick bath.
please keep your eyes on the babies, and i will be out
quickly. i just want a few moments ALONE."

will, absorbed in a newspaper, nodded his head.

when i came out, fresh and quiet and rather restored, i
smelled something horrible.

"honey, what is that smell? it smells like a dirty diaper . . .
but worse." we are in a lovely hyatt, and suddenly will's
paper drops. he gets this horrified look, and i know we are
in trouble.

colson has taken off his diaper, with you-know-what in it.
it has dropped all over the room. will was so absorbed in
his reading that he had not noticed colson. rubbing it in his
hands . . . stomping in it . . . then running around the room
. . . do i need to say more? we had a catastrophe on our
hands. while will took colson into the bathroom to bathe
and shampoo him, i proceeded, once fresh and relaxed, to
crawl all over the room, picking up bits here and there and
everywhere.

getting a wet wash cloth, full of warm water and a little soap, i would squeeze it everywhere i saw and smelled something questionable. then scrub and scrub until it no longer smelled or showed in the carpet.

i had to rebathe. will was beside himself. colson giggled, and had enjoyed it immensely. we walked down to the convention center looking close to perfect, and normal. no one knew, but we did. and every hotel room we now check into makes us leery. what have all the other children, on all the other visits, done in that room? i wear socks at all times!

brandt received these letters on his first birthday—

ta ta ta

9-6-90

Dear Brandt,

You can't read this. Happy Birthday . . . here is a check for $25.00. When you can read this, ask your Mom and Dad what they did with it.

I'm telling your parents to teach you to memorize some Bible verses. When you know what memorize means, you should be able to say: "Rejoice Always."

We love you,

Grandpa Brandt

ta ta ta

Dear Brandt,

Happy Birthday! We love you. We love your smile, too—Great.
Come see us in Florida, and you can say your Bible verses!
"God is love." Jesus loves you and your Grandma Jo does too.

5. *new hope*

more and more, will and i felt it was time for me to stay home more. to withdraw from such a focus in the public arena.

my children will be young only once. the sweet hours with them will pass so quickly, and i can never get them back. it became such a priority to us to create more of a serene surrounding for all of us. a woman can do lots of things at once, but something gets cheated. each woman must choose. i make no judgments. will and the children just fell right under my First Love, ahead of everything else.

at one point, i flew to jim and shirley dobson's. years ago, before focus on the family, i remember when jim threw in the towel of the hectic, speaking arena, and decided to stay closer to home. focus on the family developed out of that.

once, long ago, we were driving down a street in pasadena. i was in the back seat. jim pulled over to the curb, looked at shirley and me, and began to share what the Holy Spirit had been showing him. it was a moment i had never forgotten. now, with a family myself, i felt a compulsion in the same direction.

"the road" had been such a part of my life. it was almost as natural as breathing. until one has travelled for years . . . slept in hotel rooms . . . felt the joy and great responsibility

and, at times, humility of that arena, it is hard to understand the stress it really creates.

the more i withdrew from speaking, however, the more the
demands came to do speaking dates. the juiciest plums
were dangled in front of my nose.

it was easy to say, "the world needs this message . . . this
vision." ultimately, Jesus can do ANYTHING with or without us. i am not indispensible in His Cause. i must never
flatter myself so. what He really wants is a yielded spirit
and a contrite heart.

the world makes it very hard to find value in being a
mother, though it is the hardest, most challenging thing i
have ever done.

in trying to gain understanding . . . the Lord put all the
pieces together. jim and shirley were in town. i could stay
with them. dr. arch hart (*Adrenalin and Stress*) was able to
spend a couple of hours with me. leaving the children and
will, i genuinely sought Godly counsel and direction.

both jim and arch counselled will and me to go in the direction we already felt led.
simply,
eliminate as much stress as possible. build around the family. the more i would simplify, the more the world would
tempt me. but stay focused. it was all i really needed.

shortly after this divine encounter, i received a letter from a
lady who was executive director of new hope child and
family agency in seattle. she informed me they had just received licensing for the state of idaho. they were interested
in my input about open adoption.

agnes havlin, a beautiful, petite little japanese woman flew in to idaho falls with one of her key counselors, kathy. a reader of my books. a fellow dreamer. both of them full of spunk and warmth and spirit . . . and utterly God's. whatever agnes and her group did, it was quality. first class. extremely professional.

after my book, *Open Adoption,* i have had a steady flow of girls fly in from all over the country for me to help them with open adoption. some strong, committed women and families in idaho falls have become deeply involved, with will and me, in these experiences.

for several years, will and i funded thousands of dollars in phone bills and expenses to see beautiful girls and couples experience the miracle of a life surrendered . . . a baby received. . . .

to make a family somewhere. people have kept girls in their homes. participated through deliveries. been strong Christian support and immediately families.

what a thrill to have coached most of these girls through labor and delivery. i have again found the wonder and blessing of God's plans being so much better. and so full of surprises.

our little sons share in the celebration of each event as we gather in our large living room to hold small dedication services, and bond together before birth mothers and adoptive couples begin to move on down the road.

taylor, brock, colson, and brandt love the girls. watch their tummies grow. jump up and down, begging to hold each baby when it comes. we are a baby family!

this process of adoption made us a family. it constantly covers us as a team, with faithful warmth and light.

offering me the position of executive director of new hope for idaho, i suddenly found myself surrounded by support. as did my volunteers. it meant a lot to will and me not to stand alone.

agnes sent a computer. we hired a great lady, celeste, with a master's in social work, to be the social worker. to give us credibility. to begin to lift the load from me, and all who have so faithfully helped us.

anne pierson, sort of the grandmother of the pro-life movement, had often mentioned to me about agnes and her group. now the timing was perfect, and God united us.

i wish i could tell about each girl. about audrey and jenny, my first two under new hope. they . . . each one . . . are so dear to me. so like my own. a part of me wanted to take every one of those babies home with me.

as in *Open Adoption,* if there is a girl who needs someone to talk to . . . if you are reading this right now and you feel very alone, please write me: ann, 545 shoup ave. idaho falls, id 83402

i read and answer every single letter myself. though i am now working with new hope, i still personally care for each girl. we do not function as a detached agency.

> if we could see beyond today as
> God can see . . .
> if all the clouds should roll away,

the shadows flee.
o'er present griefs . . . we would not fret . . .
for many joys are waiting yet . . .
for you and me.

sometimes, to remain true to our First Love, God allows us to experience consequences. to forgive . . . to be utterly forgiven . . . but to relinquish some very dear, sacred place in us. in adoption, it is different for each girl. God speaks to and deals with each one separately. sometimes, He calls them to release that beautiful, tiny bundle. the cost is great. the reward, though, outweighs, by far, the sacrifice. we must make First Love our hope, our goal. then all the other pieces will fall into place.

a letter from my friend, agnes, at new hope.

Very Dearest Ann,

Thank you for not taking my expressions of love lightly—which is so very deep and entirely out of character for me to express.

May you always feel my love and approval and appreciation and especially the Lord's.

You are incredibly special!

                                        Agnes

6. *hawaii*

when brandt was a couple of months old, his generous
birthfather arranged for sarah to come to california to be
with me where i was speaking, and then to spend a couple
of days at the beverly hills hotel. i had eight-month-old colson. our time was delightful. we walked around, each with a
baby. blond sarah carried brandt, her baby, with black hair
and dark eyes. i toted colson. blond and blue-eyed. we
would tell people our story as we walked. they were in awe!

when brandt was about nine or ten months, i decided i
must go to hawaii to see my father and mother. as old as
my father was, i felt if i did not, i might miss him on earth
again. i love him so much . . . my ultimate spiritual mentor.

a couple of weeks before i left, i awakened in the night.
there was not handwriting on the wall, but i felt an idea
keenly. maybe sarah would like to fly to los angeles and
keep brandt there while i flew on to hawaii with jan, my
sister, for a week. on one hand, the idea startled me. on the
other, it seemed so beautiful and special. it would give
sarah eight days in little brandt's life that she would never
again have.

"sarah, it's ann," i called. "i feel God spoke to me in the
night about an idea. when i talked to will about it, he was
open. how would you feel about keeping brandt for a week
while i go with jan to hawaii, to see my parents? will is

going to keep the other three. i was going to take brandt, but it might be *so fun* for you! what do you think?"

"ann," she gasped, "are you serious? i mean, even if it does not work, i will never ever forget your thinking of this."

"will thinks you should talk to your parents. seek Godly counsel. consider it. ponder whether it would be too hard for you to let him go after eight days. but sarah, we would find so much joy in sharing him with you. he is too little to know, but you would so enjoy him, he is such a beautiful sweetheart."

it seemed beyond sarah's comprehension that we would offer her this. i felt excitement and deep joy for her.

after much prayer and consideration, sarah called. the birthfather was so generous as to allow sarah the opportunity, and her family was enthusiastic. she and her sister, and her little three-year-old niece, would come to los angeles and meet my plane. while jan and i flew on, they would stay at the beverly hills hotel and play.

i deboarded with darling brandt in one arm, in lace and curls, and his little bag in the other. there stood sarah, my exquisite birthmom and her sister and child whom i really love. handing my baby over, kissing and hugging both him and sarah, i delivered my little, happy chunk in her arms, with his bag, and boarded the flight for honolulu with jan, who had just landed from cleveland.

fearful? never. sad? no. excited beyond words for sarah and brandt.

holding what one most loves in open hand. not hanging on
or possessive. knowing the gift was God's and will always
be God's. joyful because sarah was. relaxed to enjoy my sister and parents without four sets of little hands needing
something. with three whose diapers needed changing.

in eight days, after an unforgettable time in hawaii, jan and
i stepped off our plane to find sarah, with little brandt,
tanned and smocked and fresh, in her arms. he threw himself at me. oh, i was happy to see him. i had terribly missed
all my children. for at least thirty minutes, his curly head
never moved from where he had nestled it under my chin.
he seemed so thrilled to have me back.

jan and i spent a night with sarah, and her very special sister and darling little daughter. i put brandt in his crib
when i knew he was tired (we had a suite at the beverly
hills hotel . . . thanks to the birthfather). he awakened in
the night, and i carried him to bed with me, and laid him
on my tummy, and rubbed his back until he fell asleep.

"ann," sarah smiled, "*you* are his mother. it is so obvious.
you know just what he needs. how to calm him. he loves
you so much. he missed you. without my sister helping . . .
i don't know what i would have done."

the next morning, when we parted, there were many tears
for sarah and me. i loved her so. partly my child, too. reminded of her sparkle and shining eyes every time i saw
them in my son's. she cried in love and gratitude, i think,
for me. she cried, not because she wanted to undo what
she had done in giving brandt to us, but because she loved
him, and the days had been so special. memories no one
and nothing could ever take away from where they were
locked in her heart.

we were the mothers of a priceless, small life. we were
bound together forever. it was okay to cry.

for eight days, brandt was a little king. sunning and being
strolled around beverly hills and the beautiful del coronado hotel on coronado island. he had ice cream and
splashed in the pacific.

when he was born (as with my others), the hours were so
brief in the hospital. the birthmother goes on, but the baby
remains sort of a mystery. moments like these give her
time to embrace her child. the little pieces of personality,
that are like her or her mom's. the fun and funny, hidden
pieces of his or her disposition. a time to really say hello,
and good-bye. to speak to her child in her own way . . . unknown except to God. a way that leaves her with more
peace. more comfort. more release.

sarah saved every letter i have ever written to her . . . since
before i was married and she was a child/teenager. i am
sharing a few.

ta ta ta

may 4, 1981

430 lewis wharf
boston, mass.

dear sarah,

oh, what a special young lady you are! i was amazed by your ma-
turity for sixteen . . . deeply touched by your warmth and love.
thank you for writing me!

i am getting married, and my fiance is wonderful. his name is
will anderson, from idaho falls, idaho. city girl moves to the wild
west! smile. God is so good.

when you talked about the "ruts" in life, they will always be
there. sigh. but remember, God is bigger and as you trust Him
more each day, the ruts won't seem quite so overwhelming.

i love you.
we stand together in Jesus' Name in the world.
don't forget!

> with joy,
>
> ann kiemel

ᴥ ᴥ ᴥ

february 10, 1988

545 shoup
idaho falls, idaho

my dear sarah,

i was so touched by your letter. by your honesty. all your questions and fears are so normal for someone in your position (pregnant). you really do need time to go through each option. God
will show you the RIGHT decision. there is ONE right one. make
it entirely around what is best for the baby. if it is right for the
baby (whatever that is), then it will be right for you, too. taylor is
almost four. brock almost three. last saturday, our third little son
was born. *beautiful* birth mother, 18, who flew in two-and-a-half
weeks before.

if you should decide to adopt, will and i would seriously consider your baby. one who would be close in age to colson (our
new son). taylor and brock are such great friends. so close. we
would love colson to have a sibling real close in age to him.

we *love* babies. all of us. if you choose to keep your baby, you are
old enough, and i know you could do it.

please know i am committed to you.
will stand by you.
no matter what.
it is a *personal* decision.
only you and God can make it.
God will not ever fail you.
ever! *obedience* is the secret.

i love you very much, and i know you will laugh again.
"you will know the Truth,
and the Truth will set you free."

ann kiemel anderson

⁊⁊ ⁊⁊ ⁊⁊

august 29, 1988

11 p.m. to sarah in
idaho falls, idaho

my dear sarah,

my little boys are all asleep.
how sweet and fun they have been today.
will is on the phone to africa.

my heart is so full, i have just
reread oswald chambers for today.

"faith must be tested, because it can be
turned into a personal possession only
through conflict.

"believe steadfastly on Him, (God) and all
you come up against will develop your
faith.

"faith is unutterable trust in God.
trust which never dreams that He will
not stand by us."

oh, sarah, how perfect for you right now, and
how deeply i claim it for you.

your little son will be born any day now, and *so* many things
touch me. that you were ever in my audience in dallas three
years ago, when brock was only three weeks old. that i was
drawn to personally answer your letter in '81. that i have
watched you say a complete "yes" to Jesus. i see the profound
change in you.

i will stand beside you the rest of your life. cheering and screaming for you. allowing God to help me unfold your destiny.

sarah, if you ever think of something you want for the baby . . .
an idea for his care . . . i would love to know.

i am in utter awe that you really love me and trust me. only God
could have put that in your heart.

i will never again eat peppermint . . . or peppermint-and-choco-
late-chip ice cream without thinking of you.

i will always think of you when i sit on a beach and sun. or ride
a horse-drawn wagon. or eat soup and a sandwich in a little
shop anywhere.

and many other things.

sarah, you are beautiful. so extremely intuitive and artistic and articulate on paper. God has plans for you!

oh, yes . . . i will always think of you when i see a kitty or a hamster.

thank you for coming to hear me speak, over and over. for reading my simple books. for embracing will and me as prospective parents. for the touching cards and notes.

i take your hand.
i run down the path beside you.
i will always carry bandaids to put on your heart. and clean socks when your spirits are down and soggy. i will check over my shoulder every mile . . . and more . . . to see if you need a cold drink. or more food or nourishment.

i will always *believe* that this glorious, incredible, indescribably-kind-and-generous Savior has bright, happy tomorrows for you.

He . . . nor i . . . will just love you when you are good or on target. i will do whatever is in my power, directed by God, to get you over the tough, agonizing places.

i pledge my love and life, in Jesus' Name, to rearing your baby. what intense joy and awe that you are sharing your child with us.

will and i pledge to inspire him with your love for him. your courage to release him to God.

it's almost midnight.
my heart is so full.
for will and the children and
you and my other birthmothers.

goodnight, my child . . . for i
truly feel you *are* my child.

belonging to one of the deepest,
purest places in me.

this race is almost over.
then you will be on an even
greater, more awesome assignment.
you will see.

with a quiet, beautiful song
in my heart . . . a peace and serenity.
because of Jesus.
run your race to win!
you and Jesus and love.

you CAN!
you CAN!
never give up!

forever, your loving friend and more.

                                        ann

                    ❧ ❧ ❧

sarah,

thank you for my son. his liquid brown, shining eyes. his smile
that is just like yours. his happy spirit.

i am overwhelmed.
i am touched beyond words.
i love you.
the entire andersons bless
you for our joy.

with melted heart,

                                        ann

❧ ❧ ❧

dear sarah,

i love you so!
i stood in the kitchen
and cried after you hung up.
i was overwhelmed by the gift of
brandt. i call him my little china doll.

we took all four boys shopping.
dressed up. squealing and clapping.
a *darling* sight. then to pizza hut.

you are a part of me wherever i go.

                              xoxo ann

❧ ❧ ❧

my dear sarah,

i loved hearing your voice last night.
process will lead you to God's next assignment.
oswald chambers says,
"God not only expects me to do His will.
but He is in me to do it."

                         deep love, ann

❧ ❧ ❧

dear sarah,

today i look at brandt, and i see
your spirit. your liquid eyes. your
melting charm.

today, just follow Jesus' command,
"ABIDE IN ME!"

it is so serene. do not try to
figure anything out. or beat yourself
for not being more decisive.
just ABIDE!

                                    my love, ann

                    ❧ ❧ ❧

my dearest sarah,

you were more real on the phone
than i have ever known you to be.

brandt has the dearest disposition.
yet he is not a pushover.
he is strong. persistent. determined.
he has to be. the youngest of four.

"tis so sweet to trust in Jesus.
just to take Him at His Word.
just to rest upon His promise . . ."

my arms are wrapped around your
heart. my feet in step beside you.

                                    ann
                                    proverbs 3:15

                    ❧ ❧ ❧

my dearest sarah,

i hold little brandt's head in
my hand. overwhelmed by this
miracle. only God's great love

could have given us brandt, colson,
brock, and taylor!

words seem dumb . . . empty . . . worthless . . .
in trying to tell you what i feel.
i think of your poise and courage
through labor and delivery.

my desk is covered. my phone
is ringing. ringing. people stopping.
three other little mouths to feed.
i must run.

i carry your spirit as i carry
little brandt.
and i send up a thousand
balloons for you!

Jesus never fails!

                                        ann

                    ❧ ❧ ❧

these private notes saved by sarah, my most recent
birthmother, describe my love . . . and God's . . . that runs
from my heart, and His, to her and my other three. without
these courageous women, i would never be called
"mommy." our home would be empty and bare and too
neat. i would be living with gaping holes that God has
tucked each little baby into.

but i do not worship my birthmothers or my husband or
my sons. they are magnificent gifts. treasures. literally a
part of my every breath and thought and sigh. but . . .

only God is the Hero. only His Lordship do i worship. He
created them and me. and life is a fleeting breath. eternity
is forever. He may take them or give more. they will bring
me great joy and devastating sorrow. He uses them in my
life, and i in theirs.

my ultimate love and trust must be in Him. He is my
Focus. my Source of joy and peace and contentment.

"oh, Jesus, please help me to never embrace will or my children or the birthmothers . . . or places or things . . . more
than i embrace You!"

a constant challenge. a daily prayer. my imperfect life . . .
that wants to cling to and possess those i most love.

"Father, forgive me."

7. the move

our house had been on the market for almost a year. i never knew selling one's house could be such a major personal, consuming adventure.

will and i had bought the brand new home on laguna street before we were married so it would be waiting for us after the honeymoon. we loved the house. modern. open. all-tile kitchen and bath. white wall-to-wall carpet throughout the entire house. utterly fresh and clean.

suddenly, with four little boys, the house shrank. we desperately needed more space (we thought). my mother-in-law had married dr. henry brandt, a christian world renowned child and family counselor. he had a beautiful condominium on the atlantic in west palm beach, florida . . . that left the sprawling "home place" with forty acres, lots of trees, and corral, and massive picture windows exposing miles of sky and mountain range, in idaho.

my mother-in-law . . . and all the family . . . really did not want to lose this wonderful house stuffed with years of memories. it was suggested that will and i buy it, and our enthusiasm mounted with every couple who came to look at our present house.

i took it very personally when interested buyers found something that was not quite right for them . . . or never

called to even say . . . "no . . . we aren't interested in your
house."

will and i had picked this house out. had loved it. felt it
was beautiful. will had planted several dozen trees that
grew quickly . . . while i had wallpapered, hung pictures
and recovered the sofas.

it looked like a sun valley setting. a home that fit close to
some ski slopes.

previously, i had sold my condominium on the waterfront
of boston (the first day), and a condominium i had bought,
outside san francisco, for my mom and dad who, as preach-
ers, had NEVER owned a home. that sold within a few
days, also. i received twice as much on each condominium
in the sales.

naturally, i was excited and ready to sell on laguna. my
past experience told me it would be a snap. we could very
soon fix up the home place and make the transition.

God had done an amazing thing in my heart. originally, i
had said i would NEVER move to the home place. never.
never. it was three miles beyond the city limits. it was the
country, and that was foreign to me.

it did have a wonderful floor plan, with a huge cathedral
ceiling living room that will's dad had added on twenty
years ago. an outstanding architect from salt lake city had
designed it.

a massive fireplace. an entire wall of windows from ceiling
to floor, overlooking the acreage and mountains in the dis-

tance. and dark, wide-plank floors that were beautiful and unusual.

regardless, it had not been redone in years, and i always liked things that were brand new. clear. fresh. modern country. even though the home place was filled with many memories, and lots of big trees and yard (besides the forty acres) for little boys to play in . . . i wanted to build . . . in a nice neighborhood . . . and do it all my way.

however, one night . . . late . . . we were driving home from sun valley. out of seemingly thin air, i began to formulate an idea for the home place.

what if guy and karleen (the sharpest builder-decorator team, i thought, in our area) helped us redo the house? what if we took the bulk of the money we made on our last house to do this? i loved the feeling they created in a home.

a couple weeks later, i took karleen out to look . . . "please be honest, karleen," i shyly smiled. "really and truly, do you think this place has lots of potential? that we could really make it ours? freshen it up. make it bright and open?"

karleen loved the house. guy said they were willing to oversee the remodeling and fixing up. i was ECSTATIC!

now, though, when was our house going to sell?

a realtor would call unexpectedly. "i have a couple seriously interested in your house. can i bring them by at 2 p.m.?"

will and i had gone over with the realtors that we did not want just everyone traipsing through. we had drawn certain parameters as guidelines. couples with no more than two children. someone who did not mind the laundry room downstairs off the playroom. anyone who did not have a massive hutch for the dining room because there was no place for one.

when you have four little boys, four and under, it is too hard making it perfect for people who would not be serious contenders.

2 p.m.

someone coming to look at the house. it was now 1 p.m.

i would fly into orbit. fixing the cribs. straightening all the beds. totally cleaning off the tile kitchen counter. lining up all the little boys' shoes perfectly. scouring the bathrooms. taylor and brock helping pick up all the toys in the playroom. nothing in the sink. nothing on the kitchen and bath counters. the sofa pillows puffed up and replaced. certain lamps turned on, even in daylight. the garage hosed down. all the toys out of the backyard. the sandbox completely straightened.

can you imagine accomplishing this with four little boys following you around, wanting to undo everything you have just done?

my final job was to put all four of the little boys in their carseats. hook them in with bottles or a toy. i would go back into the house and vacuum every inch, stepping behind the vacuum in such a way that no footprints showed ANYWHERE. quite a feat, especially when you have to get the vacuum back into the closet, and your body to the garage.

somehow, i KNEW it was my job to sell this house. if it was perfect enough, people would beg to buy it.

that was a terrible assumption, totally doomed for defeat. flying out the garage . . . clicking the garage door down, i would hurry out of the drive seconds before the realtor pulled in. taylor, brock, colson, and brandt . . . and i . . . would drive around and around the block and neighborhood, praying THIS family would want to buy the house.

we made sure the realtor called us after each visit just so we could know the responses, and not hang in uncertainty.

every time someone came to see the house, i worked and cleaned as if i *knew* this was the buyer. the children would clap their hands and believe, too. and with every "no" i personally felt rejected. unloved. unqualified.

a borderline misfit.

taylor and brock prayed every day. "dear Jesus, please help SOMEONE to buy our house."

the routine got old very fast. i hesitated every time the phone rang. yet, if several days went by, and NO ONE showed interest, i felt completely defective and pathetic. one's house is truly a part of one's identity. in our neighborhood, there were several houses for sale. we began to celebrate every time a house sold. we had a sense of camaraderie. of joint success. if the house down the street sold, the rest of us were in awe. our hopes were bouyed, too, for ourselves.

if will was home during the preparation for the realtor's visit, i drove him to distraction.

"honey! do not walk on that side of the carpet! it is perfect.
i just vacuumed all the footprints."

at one juncture, i had my faithful carpet cleaning man
come to brighten all the rug area. wall-to-wall white carpet
with four little boys is basically impossible. i am sure i was
his number one customer. at least every six or seven weeks,
i had him over to clean.

the little boys loved the big, orange hoses and the loud
sucking noises. the carpet cleaner was one of their heroes.

the carpets were spotless and ready for the next house
showing, when i decided that very afternoon, after they
were cleaned, to fix a big pot of chili.

pulling out the piping-hot, homemade cornbread from the
oven, i proceeded to fill all the bowls with chili so they
could cool a little.

quickly i flipped on the television in the living room to see
if any major news stories were being aired.

holding a bowl of chili in one hand, i reached out to pick
up the remote control. taylor, completely distracted and
looking in the opposite direction, crashed into me, and the
full bowl of chili flew out of my hand, upside down on the
just shampooed white carpet.

i stood in shock and horror. i could not move. i could not
even get a noise out of my throat. i only stared, numbly, at
chili . . . hamburger, tomato sauce, onion . . . strewn from
one wall of carpet to the other.

taylor burst into tears, after which i did. we stood there, side-by-side, our arms around each other in frozen disbelief.

"darling," i finally squeaked out, "it was an accident. it really was. mommy understands."

the babies were crawling around in wide-eyed delight, smearing the chili with their fingers, and brock sat down, right where he was, staring with his huge, liquid-brown eyes.

grabbing the phone, i dialed paul's cleaning. "paul, you would not believe what just happened." i sobbed. "i spilled an entire bowl of chili all over the middle of the living room carpet."

"paul," i continued, crying uncontrollably, "i am sure it is ruined. you will never be able to get this stuff out."

he could not help but laugh.

"ann, blot it up as best you can with a damp towel, and i will come first thing tomorrow morning and get it out."

there are few things more humbling than trying to sell your house for a full year. i began to truly understand that only Jesus could do it. our house was in a price range above where many were looking and a size accommodation for only certain families.

one day, our realtor, nancy, called.

"i have the perfect couple to look at your house, ann, when can i bring them by?"

"you can't! nancy, today i do not care if we EVER sell this house. today, i do not have it in me to show it."

"ann . . . please . . . "

"no, nancy, i mean it. putting all four children in the car and vacuuming all the footprints is more than i can handle!"

the children were all taking naps, and i was propped in bed, having my devotions. suddenly, i heard a soft knock. looking up, there stood nancy.

"what do you want me to do, ann? show me where the vacuum is and i will start on the other end of the house."

that is a realtor! no wonder she was number one in idaho. how can a seller say "no" to that!

the people that day did not buy the house. my second day home after the abscess surgery, a couple weeks later, it sold.

my beautiful mother-in-law was there, and when she heard me say "no" again to the realtor, she began nodding her head.

"ann . . . we can do it. i will do it."

"no, jo," i cried. white and trembling and weak. she persisted, and i succumbed.

my dear friend, roxanne, brought her vacuum over, because i was not allowed to push a vacuum. jo headed for the garage. i helped the children pick up toys, cleaned the bathroom sinks, and cleared the deck.

that day in august, 1989, i was too weak and in pain to feel anything but a desperate longing to survive for will and the children.

however, that day, the new navy dentist in town . . . a world-traveled bachelor . . . came to see the house, and fell in love with it. God's timing is so unpredictable. humanly, i would have thought any other week would be better to sell.

i sat in a corner, against the wall, while our wonderful church body came in, packed, and completely moved us out to the home place. because this dentist wanted in immediately, will felt we should go ahead and move directly to the big house. the work would be done on it while we lived there.

it was very hard saying good-bye to all our neighbors. especially the children next door. the two little boys, tanner and tyson, were taylor's and brock's favorite buddies. the one daughter, tanielle, was such a help with my babies.

i remember my father and mother saying i should never hold too tightly to people or places or things. only hold onto Jesus. that if i put too much value on a person or a place, i might fail to do God's will. to be resilient in it. to march boldly to His drum for my life.

one of the most difficult experiences i can ever remember was moving into the country home with nothing having been done on it. very weak and sick from surgery and the morphine withdrawal. and four little boys, still really babies, to care for.

unpacking boxes was incomprehensible to me. i had
wanted more space, but this house was twice as big, at
least, as our former one.

suddenly, the smaller home seemed so new and fresh and
warm and cozy compared to this house. my babies weren't
just down the hall.

there were painters all over the outside of the house, putting a fresh coat of white paint on the outside, and repaint-
ing all the black shutters. inside, workmen were drilling
out the white rock in the entry. painters were painting
every room on the inside. wallpaper was being hung deli-
cately in areas. blond plank flooring was going in the entry
and entire kitchen area. the kitchen ceiling being lowered.
new appliances and counter tops and floors in kitchen and
baths. new carpet being laid throughout. a new bannister
for the stairs.

will had to make a quick business trip to washington, d.c.,
and i decided to take all four of the children on a speaking
trip with me. upon arriving home, exhausted, friends
picked the children and me up and dropped us at the
house. i thanked them profusely, waved good-bye, and
closed the door.

going into the master bedroom, i saw the king-sized bed
was piled with boxes and furniture while they had laid all
new carpet. there was no way i could unload all of that.

"children," i announced, "go get in the car in the garage."

piling our bags directly into the car trunk, i turned out all
the lights, locked everything, and headed for shilo inn, the

beautiful, new hotel in town. we would just stay there, i decided, for a couple nights until will returned.

a baby in each arm, and taylor and brock carrying small
bags, we stumbled to our first floor room at the shilo. it
seemed rather strange to me that policemen were roaming
up and down the halls and outside the doors.

on my second trip to the room, with more bags, i walked
over to one of the officers.

"excuse me, sir, but is there some reason you are roaming
around the hall?"

"uh-yes, there is. a 'peeping tom' has been disturbing
guests and we have not been able to catch him, yet."

a peeping tom? i could not have cared less.

if the curtains were closed and the door locked, it seemed
to me we were safe. i was SO GLAD to be out of that big
house strewn with workmen and electricians and painters
and boxes.

it was extremely difficult to live through renovation, weak
from miscarriage and surgery, with four children as small
as ours were. they were not allowed to touch the outside or
the inside of the house. they heard almost nothing but,

"oh, darling, do not step there!" and, "no, brock, you cannot ride your tricycle on the road. i know there are no sidewalks out here, so you will have to stay in the circular
drive."

"taylor!" i screamed. "where are brandt and colson? i had them dressed and perfect for church and i cannot find them anywhere."

"mommy, they crawled into the corral, and are playing in some mud."

I solemnly promise . . . before everyone who ever reads this book . . . that i will NEVER EVER AGAIN move into a house before the renovation is complete!

but Jesus saw us through. faithful, faithful Savior. my best friend.

today the house is perfect for us. large and roomy and airy. there are things i still long to do . . . when we have more money to spend on it. some imperfections (smile) but *it is so perfect for us.* God's timing is just right, too.

8. hysterectomy

following the july surgery, i lived in pain. i had experienced so many pregnancies, miscarriages, abdominal infections. my resistance was, at that point, so low that i picked up every bug my children got, and my abdomen was full of adhesions.

the outside incision always healed beautifully. a tiny, thin line. hardly noticeable. my problem was massive adhesions on the inside. compounded, by the fact that i had incredible resistance to medication.

when i was a child, the dentist had to give me four shots to numb my gums. he told my mother that i was the most resistant person to medication that he had ever worked with. after my first miscarriage, they wheeled me in for a D and C. the ob-gyn laughed afterwards.

"ann, you are so little . . . so petite. i feared i was going to kill you. i pumped enough anesthesia in you to kill a three hundred pound man. you would keep waking up, thinking i was your agent. you kept telling me to cancel another speaking date."

i realized, more and more, that a hysterectomy was inevitable. with four little sons . . . more wonderful and special than i could ever have dreamed . . . and a strong, exciting husband, health became far more my focus than personally delivering a baby, and proving to the world i was not defective.

with two major speaking appearances in september, i scheduled the hysterectomy for early october. with jim, the ob-gyn i trusted implicitly, i waited for that dreaded, fateful moment. i had smugly promised i would NEVER succumb to . . . a hysterectomy. i prayed that either my pain would go away, or i would conceive so as to spare me another major surgery, and having my womanhood, i thought, confiscated.

at that moment, after years of fighting infertility, i had lost my health. until that happens, one has no idea of the panic and devastation that creates in one's heart.

would my little boys ever have a full-fledged mom again? would i ever be strong enough to raise them in a normal, healthy environment? my anguish was beyond comprehension. my fear paralyzing.

the night before my hysterectomy, i insisted they do a pregnancy test. God could still spare me from the surgery. a powerful, catholic-charismatic couple came to my room and prayed for me. their love and spirit remain unforgettable in my mind.

an anesthetist, who had assisted in epidurals for my pregnant girls, volunteered to cover my anesthesia for the surgery. a new procedure was decided on . . . to give me a spinal, so i would not have to go under . . . the thing i feared most.

with the pregnancy test negative, they rolled me toward the swinging doors and bright lights of surgery. i knew i was relinquishing, forever, the possibility of carrying a

baby and delivering . . . and receiving what i thought was
the good housekeeping seal of approval as a woman.

i was so terrified of pain. i wondered how a woman could
possibly do this without four beautiful little sons to go
home to? some women had no children to go home to. no
relevant hope of motherhood. oh, people can be so
courageous.

the recovery room was one of my most dreaded experiences. i often would shake and tremble. i would feel so
fuzzy, so powerless. i would moan that i was in pain and
they would pat my hand and tell me they had given me
something ten minutes earlier. it wasn't enough, but i was
too zonked and anesthetized to assert myself, and
DEMAND more relief. usually, i could hear others around
me, moaning and groaning.

all my life, i had been so healthy. i do not remember my
mother even sticking a thermometer in my mouth. even
having one in my house. these past few years of infertility-
pregnancy struggle had left me completely depleted of
strength, and my spirit hanging onto the edge for dear life.

the anesthesiologist and anesthetist were shocked at what it
took to keep me comfortable, even though i had told them
what childhood doctors had warned me of . . . extreme resistance to medication. being 5' 8" and 112 lbs., they feared
they would kill me. finding a balance was difficult. one
minute i would be in agony; the next, i would almost stop
breathing.

some beautiful Christian nurses sat at my bedside the first
twenty-four hours just to keep an eye on me.

this was my second major surgery in two months, following a miscarriage . . . after nine or ten major surgeries in
the past nine years. all related to pregnancy.

by the time the hysterectomy was over, i had no strength,
nothing left to grieve. months and years of grieving had
evolved. now my only grief was being so physically broken. would i ever see my little boys grow up? would i ever
be truly normal again? feel healthy and strong? until you
completely lose your health, you cannot imagine the terror
and desperate longing for life. after the morphine withdrawal in the last operation, i was also CERTAIN i would
not allow that to happen again!

will would bring the four little boys to the hospital room.
they would snuggle next to me in bed. lie quietly and hold
my hand. we would softly talk and share. i lived for their
visits . . . and was exhausted when it was time for them to
leave. burying my head in the pillow, i would sob. i was so
lonely for will and the children. for my own bed. i had
seen so many hospital rooms . . . been poked so many
times. felt so utterly defective.

"oh, Jesus, can i ever be normal again?" i pleaded. "can i
do the laundry? can i cook? can i EVER walk around,
doing simple chores? can i feel decent and normal like everyday people?"

in a week, will brought me home. i had a regular pharmacy there . . . pain medicine, antibiotics, some kind of
tranquilizer. i gave the medicine to will and said, "only
give me something when i REALLY need it." the thought
of drug withdrawal was the most terrifying consideration
of all.

there were a few humorous moments. first of all, we were still in the midst of renovation. i am a perfectionist . . . and the house was still so IMPERFECT!

our dear friend, dot, flew in and took over the cooking and children for two weeks. penny, another great friend, did the next two weeks. can you imagine such love? four little boys to dress and feed and keep clean. laundry to catch up on. walks in the stroller in crisp, cold october days down country roads. babies' cheeks rosy and eyes glistening.

all the while, i lay in our bed, barely able to lift my head off the pillow. will would allow the children to file in several times a day. lined up by the bed . . . the babies resting their chins on the mattress, lifting their liquid eyes to me sadly.

never before . . . never . . . in my life did i have to battle this raging fear and terror that i was not going to come out of it.

within three weeks, i was off all medications. i never took the tranquilizer, and felt absolutely no withdrawal from my other medication. one morphine experience is enough for an entire lifetime.

dot and penny were the most incredible people. they gave of their own energy and time. they took no money. they served in the most humble, caring way. every meal, they would walk into my closed-doors' bedroom, with something wonderful on a tray. i will never ever forget it. running around after four little boys . . . and their daddy . . . doing laundry . . . keeping the house clean and in order . . .

wore them both out. they returned to their respective cities, and crashed, i believe, for days.

i longed for my moments with the children. then i begged for complete rest and solitude. many tears soaked my pillow. there is NOTHING as scary (that i know) as fearing you WILL NEVER be strong again. strong enough to watch your small sons grow up. i loved them more than life. completely losing my health brought me to the very last point in the road. to the utter, absolute end of myself.

i cannot remember will ONCE complaining. he moved his office (partially) home. his computer and phone line. a desk. he basically existed in his little office here at our house so he could change the babies' diapers. put them down for their naps. help the women feed and bathe them. he appeared at my slightest call. he took taylor to kindergarten. read books to all the little ones. he continually promised that i would make it. he could laugh when all i could do was cry. he was my husband, the father of our children. the breadwinner. we all knew we could count on him, we treasured his optimism and joy.

never had i known terror like the fears that engulfed me the first month post-op. i could not pick up my babies. or climb stairs. or lift anything. or push a vacuum. where once i had resiliently run ten fast miles every morning, i now could only make it to the bathroom and back to bed.

would my children grow up warped? every day, taylor and brock prayed, "dear Jesus . . . please make mommy better."

by the sixth week, i began to think, "i can make it." an exhilarating prospect. I felt good. very weak, but no pain.

NO PAIN! it seemed incomprehensible! it was the first time i had not had pain in several years.

and the thing i feared the very most . . . that i would go through some kind of drug withdrawal . . . never happened. Jesus delivered me. i will worship Him and honor Him forever!

there never came a time when i grieved deeply over what i lost in the hysterectomy. my grieving had sucked every desperate and sad feeling out of me for several years. my grieving was over when they wheeled me into the operating room, and i knew i had given pregnancy every chance i had. i had fought a good fight. i had finished that particular race. i could not hang on to anything that kept me from my First Love.

my grief now was over losing my health. many days, it took every ounce of courage i could muster to simply live. to breathe. to will, through the grace of Jesus, to get well. walking down the road. strolling the mall. getting the children up and caring for them just one day. those were all miracles. every tiny step was a giant victory!

one thing alone saved me. every hour of every day, i KNEW i was utterly powerless. I KNOW i could not ever come out of this hole unless Jesus miraculously rescued me. there was NOTHING i could do in my own physical or mental power to save me. every minute of every hour i cast all the faith i had EVER stored away in my private bank account on Him.

it really had nothing to do with being determined enough. all my life, i had drawn from this incredible sense of courage and drive and determination.

my marathoning was a perfect example of this. at thirty-four, with basically no athletic background, i willed myself through the rigorous training and fortitude of mile after mile after mile of training. i KNOW Jesus was the One who got me to every starting line . . . and over every finish.

Jesus gets ALL the credit for everything of any value that i have accomplished. after the hysterectomy, however, i was too weak . . . too depleted . . . too broken . . . too empty of adrenaline and vision and will power.

every moment was a miracle. and if i had allowed the evil one to slip one little, tiny toe in the door, it would have been over. i acknowledged, by the moment, my overwhelming love and devotion and commitment to Jesus. i confessed, over and over, what i was not . . . and embraced constantly all the promises of victory through Him.

in one's journey, human expectations can seem dashed and obliterated. dreams shattered into millions of tiny pieces. a marriage that may not be what you had always dreamed it would be. a handicapped child. paralysis. cancer. hysterectomy. never making a million dollars.

it does not have to . . . and must not . . . alter one's First Love. our First Love can flourish and blossom and radiate and capture hope and joy and peace and long suffering and kindness and genuinely-authentic love.

there were so many gifts and joys i had . . . but the hysterectomy, once and for all, resolved and decided for me the
inability of my personally carrying and delivering a baby.
of will and my sharing in that sacred, unique creation.
though i have been pregnant, i have never felt a baby kick.
i will never deliver my own baby.

but NOTHING could be more like my own flesh than taylor, brock, colson, and brandt. not for an instant would will
and i trade one of our priceless sons for any we have lost.
we could never have done it as well . . . not even close . . .
as God did it through the four we have.

🙟 🙟 🙟

I will not doubt though sorrows fall
    like rain,
and troubles swarm like bees about a hive.
I will believe the heights for which
    I strive are only revealed
    by anguish and by pain;
and though I groan and writhe beneath
    my crosses,
I yet shall see through my severest losses,
the greater gain.

(Unknown author)

Prison, I love you. You have been good to me.

(Solzhenitsyn)

Pain does not make you great. If it did, the whole world
would be great . . . because everyone has suffered . . .

(Anne Morrow Lindbergh)

but it is how you open your life to pain. what you let
Jesus do with it. it is becoming friends with pain. . . .
walking beside her . . . embracing her. many of our
greatest surprises have come from pain and suffering.

(ann k. anderson)

Whole, unbruised, unbroken men are of little use to God
. . . because they are deficient in agape love.

(J. R. Miller)

9. father's death

the seventh week, following my hysterectomy, was approached with incredible anticipation. i dreamed of picking one of my babies up. of going upstairs and rocking them, and tucking all four of them into bed.

i could taste being their real mom again. doing normal things. laughing with will as we worked together in the kitchen.

that week did come. my little boys were so happy. they all wanted me to pick them up. they insisted that i bathe them. that i pull the covers under their chins. they really and truly had a mommy! for them, it was a miracle. and for me, the simplest gestures were the most cherished. it is so easy to forget their magic!

will came in a few days before, and said, "honey, i stood in the kitchen and looked at those four little boys, and it made me teary. they were little boys without a mom. i could see it in their eyes, their spirits. ann, you give them something that not i nor anyone else but you can give."

my eyes glistened with tears as i picked up colson and brandt the first day of the seventh week. as i realized that the beautiful women had gone, and this really was my house . . . my domain. i was in charge. do you have ANY idea what that meant to me after several months of not having it? i tasted beauty in the smallest things. getting brandt

a cup of juice. tying brock's shoes. holding taylor's hand
and climbing the stairs to bed with him. fixing hot muffins
for colson.

the second day of the seventh week, our phone rang.

"hello," i responded joyfully.

"ann, this is dr. carter, in hawaii. your dad is terribly sick
and if you do not come NOW i fear you will never see him
alive again!"

my holy, little father. my major spiritual mentor. the one
who had most prayed me through these dark, prison experiences. i knew i could ALWAYS call any hour of the day
or night, and he would be there, instantly, to listen and
care and pray. i was his namesake. (jan was named janet
ruth . . . ruth after my mom. being from the south, it was
rather common to give me my father's name . . . harold
ann kiemel. fred, my older brother, had been named after
our grandfather.)

for years, i dreaded the first day of school. all the forms to
fill out. last name. first name. middle initial. even though
we were always called "ann and jan," i had to be honest,
on the forms, and at roll call, the teacher ALWAYS announced "harold kiemel." i would raise my hand to show i
was present, and who that name belonged to.

"no, honey, i said HAROLD kiemel!" the teacher would
oddly smile, and look around for a boy to claim that name.
especially in growing up in hawaii, the teachers never could
understand why i had been punished with a man's name.

i was very shy. quietly standing, i would explain: "i was named after my father, but please just call me 'ann'."

children would giggle and i would be mortified. around sixth grade, i got smart. i would put ann h. kiemel on the forms, and if they asked what the "h" stood for, i would smile and only say it was a unique family name . . . and not mention what it was.

that day when the doctor called, i had just bathed the children. shampooed everyone's head, including mine. no one had any clothes on. my wet hair was dripping in my eyes, and the babies were playing hard-to-catch as i tried to grab them and hook a diaper on.

"oh, Jesus, how can my father be dying the very first week i am really on my feet again, and finally able to be a mother?"

calling my sister and brother, i proceeded to call will and seek his counsel. i was devastated that my dad was dying. if you have really had a great relationship with a parent, you are NEVER ready for them to die. they are never old enough . . . or have lived long enough. at least that is how i felt.

"honey, my dad is dying in hawaii, and the doctor said if i do not come, i will never see him alive again," i sobbed to will, still at the office.

remember, i was soaked. my heavy hair had to be dried. of course, nothing was packed. the children huddled around me, stricken at the thought that i might leave them. the next and last flight out of idaho falls that day left in a little over one hour.

"ann, the children are resilient. i will be here for them. i can just move my office back to the house. you will never regret seeing your father one more time . . . especially since he is still coherent."

i had called my father . . . at the hospital . . . and he had said, "oh, honey, can you come?"

my dad had taught me to believe in a giant God. to let Jesus plant dreams . . . impossible ones . . . in me. to run the race to win. to always be faithful. how could i choose between him and my children? will was a strong man. i knew he would make it. i loved him so much for saying, unselfishly, "go!"

will's father had died of stomach cancer twelve years before, and will's main regret was that he had not carried his father to a car, and driven him somewhere to fly-fish one more time. his dad, a world-class fly fisherman, had taught will everything he knew about the sport. it was something they both loved.

(being a city woman, i still cannot figure out why fishing is so fun. i am often cold. according to will, the best fishing is when it rains or the wind blows. you wait for hours, sometimes, to get a catch, and maybe you do not get one at all. i do not like putting on the fat, squirming worms or pulling the hooks out of the fish's mouth while it flips and flops. fishing really is a mystery to me!)

i began to pray. "Jesus, if i am to go to see my dad, please help everything to fall into place."

jan said she could meet me in los angeles, and fly the rest of the way with me. fred, my brother, was coming the next

afternoon. our dearest friends said they would take wonderful care of the boys when will needed them to. my gyne-
cologist, jim, said i could fly, and even take my littlest
baby, brandt. everything seemed to say "go."

karleen, another friend, called and said, "what can i do to
help?"

crying, i began throwing some clothes together. (it was
early december, and hawaii would be very warm.) packing
up things for the children. suddenly, i noticed colson, one-
and-a-half, walking right into a wall, and falling back-
wards. then he walked into a door, and it threw him back.
he did not cry. he just had a sort of glassy stare on his face.
i was shocked.

dialing my children's doctor, becoming more hysterical by
the minute, i said, "sally, i know colson has had a mild
case of pneumonia, but something else is wrong. he is walking into walls as if he cannot see them. i am petrified. does
he have meningitis? my father is dying. i am to fly to hawaii. i do not know where will is . . . my hair is wet . . . "

"ann, wrap him in a blanket, and rocco (her husband, also
a physician) will meet you at the emergency room of the
hospital."

i was frantic. who would care for the children while i was
at the hospital? where was will? were we going to lose our
little son whom we loved more than life itself?

quickly, i began throwing (almost literally) clothes on my
body. i gave colson a sponge bath to freshen him up. just
stalling. where was will?

suddenly, throwing a wet diaper in the trash, i heard our car, and will came bounding in. he immediately wrapped his arms around me, and began trying to understand what the jibberish coming out of my mouth was.

as if lightning struck my brain, i looked at will, and said, "where is all that medicine they sent home with me from the hospital? where, honey?"

having given all the pills to will, while stumbling into bed, i had never even asked him where he had put them away for me. the miracle was God's planting that thought in me.

will's dark eyes flashed. he thought a moment.

"ann, i put them down in my little office, so the children would not find them."

both of us raced down the three steps to his office. we stood at the door in shocked disbelief. pills in child proof caps had been strewn everywhere!!

"colson," i commanded to my glassy-eyed child, "did you do this?"

i gave him direct eye contact . . . two inches from his little face . . . and he nodded "yes" and spoke at the same time. "uh-huh, mommy. colson play with pills."

wildly, i began to count them with will. it is obvious pills are missing. they are very small. easy to swallow. he thought they were candy, i am sure. racing to the phone, i called the doctor again. "sally, i am almost sure he has taken some of the pills that they sent home with me from the hospital."

"oh, ann, that is a relief," sally responded. "they are not as toxic as laundry detergent. just get colson to the hospital, and we will pump his stomach."

standing there, undressed, wet hair in my eyes. clinging to colson tightly, as he just sort of stared into space. i never thought i would pray for him to get through his "terrible twos," but at the moment, it seemed the most wonderful thought in the world.

"ann," will commanded quietly, "give me colson. i will head for the hospital, while you pack and go to the airport."

"honey," i sobbed, still hysterical, "i cannot leave my baby like this. i am his mother. what if he does not make it?"

every option had a terrible side. i was possibly going to miss ever talking to my father again . . . on earth . . . or being with colson and sending my priceless child to the hospital. i knew colson loved his daddy. will could handle this. BUT i had NEVER not gone to the hospital when one of the children was sick. when brandt had the croup, i crawled into his crib and under the oxygen tent with him. i did not leave his room. i held brock while they sewed stitches in his eye from falling out of his crib. when taylor was a baby, he became so ill that he lost most of his fluids. they hospitalized him to inject an i.v., and i did not leave the hospital for five days.

wrapping colson in a warm blanket, i handed him to will, saying i would call from the airport. roxanne came for taylor and brock. karleen took brandt and me to the airport.

checking in at delta airlines, i ran to a pay phone and dialed the hospital's emergency room.

"this is ann kiemel anderson. my husband brought our baby, colson, in. can you put will or rocco (doctor) on the phone?"

will spoke to me. then rocco.

"ann," rocco spoke with confidence. "colson is going to be fine. we just pumped his stomach, and no one likes that, but he is okay. i am admitting him for twenty-four hours, but will is here and will spend the night with him. you go to your dad."

"rocco," i wept, "this is not just anyone's baby. this is MY baby. i cannot get on the plane unless you promise he is going to make it, and he is content with his daddy, and not missing me too much."

there is NO love on earth, i think, as potent and enduring, as a mother's love for her child. a bear for her cubs. a horse for her colt.

with rocco and will reassuring me over and over, i hugged karleen and boarded the plane for los angeles . . . and on to hawaii. brandt cradled in my arms. colson in the hospital. seven weeks post-op. my hysterectomy. tears streamed down my face, as i "set my face like flint" to do what i finally felt God wanted.

will needs his own cherished memories with the little boys. his own rescue missions. i must constantly let go of my powerful grip on things that, ultimately, belong to Jesus.

a very hard lesson. one Jesus challenges me to learn over
and over.

jan, my sister, met my flight into los angeles (hers had just
landed from cleveland). taking turns holding my little
chunk, brandt . . . mellow, happy, darling baby . . . we flew
the tedious hours to honolulu. arriving there at 9 p.m. (midnight, my time; 2 a.m., jan's). exhausted. emotionally
sapped. the incision in my abdomen throbbing.

someone from the church picked us up. it took one hour to
cross the island of oahu to kailua, where my parents lived.
where my father, at eighty-two years, was the prayer pastor of the nazarene church there. they paid him to pray! to
intercede an hour a day for Christ's followers. and for
those who were maybe not Christ's. but were loved and
cared about.

jan and i insisted on going by the hospital, though extremely late, to see my father. we would stay with my
mom in their quaint, studio apartment.

nothing could have prepared us for the sight of my father.
ashen. tubes everywhere.

"daddy, oh, daddy," jan and i started to cry.

"ann darling . . . jan darling?" he responded, weakly.

"oh, daddy, we love you so much. you have protected us.
prayed over us. been our spiritual hero . . .

"daddy," i sobbed, continuing, "i will never be ready for
you to die."

jan and i kissed and kissed my dear, little, white-haired, holy father. we showed him brandt, his youngest grand-child. he had never seen him before.

still crying as we left the hospital, and praying Jesus would somehow spare my father through the night, we dragged baby and bags to the family studio apartment, and my beautiful mother.

my mother. my ideal. seventy-seven years old. still much of her black hair, with just streaks of gray. prodigy child pi-anist and student. now very forgetful. physically healthy and strong, but failing mentally. my father, mentally so alert and bright, with a broken, tired body.

after fourteen hours of flying, with a baby in tow. barely seven weeks post-op. the hysterectomy. i collapsed into bed, not knowing if i or my father would die first. i had checked on colson. he was doing great.

fred, our brother, was flying in the next day.

my mother, and jan and i and brandt headed for the hospital the next morning, december 4, 1989. no one, except grand-parents, had ever died in our family. how does one ever pre-pare oneself for saying "goodbye" . . . for now . . . to some-one you love so deeply? to someone so much a part of the utter essence of all you are? a part of God's whole shaping of you. to someone you hold as dear as anyone in life?

until one has lost, in death, a person this deeply loved, one cannot speak with true understanding. even today, almost a year since my father's death, i am deeply changed. for-ever quieted and humbled by life . . . and its gifts . . . and the quickness by which it can be snapped away.

my father looked even worse the next morning. i went down to the emergency room because my abdomen was hurting so terribly. i had an infection and had to be treated. but nothing could keep me from my father's bedside.

we sang . . . jan and i and my mom . . . all the old hymns my father had sung to us all our lives. i lay brandt on my father's chest.

"daddy, please pray for each of your grandchildren one more time."

he wrapped brandt into his arms, tubes tangled around both of them.

dear Lord Jesus . . .
dear Heavenly, Divine Father . . .
may Your spirit pass from me
to brandt and colson and brock and taylor. . . .
to tasha and sean paul . . .
to tre and nash and christian . . .
oh, dearest Holy Spirit . . .
deliver them from the evil one.
may the world be different because of
Your love and life in them.

a hallowed moment.
a sacred memory.

his handsome, refined doctor, came in and asked us to step out.

"i want you to know that reverend kiemel cannot make it
more than three more days. he has kidney failure. heart failure. he is a very special man, and i am very sorry the
world will lose him."

my mother, married to my father fifty-plus years, seemed
numb. jan and i wept. would fred make it before daddy
died?

no one . . . absolutely no one . . . had dominated my
father's prayers more than fred. his only son. his first born.
the child he felt he never really knew how to parent.

nurses came and went. they told us how they loved my father. that they never had cared for anyone more loving,
who suffered with such quiet poise. never complaining.

jan and i had taken a brief break. a lovely lady from the
church watched brandt down the hall. when we returned
to my father's room, he began to quote the twenty-third
psalm.

how many times had i watched my father speak that same
psalm to others, dying. share it at multiple funerals he pre-
sided over.

jan and i and mother started quoting the psalm, aloud,
with him.

"though i walk through the valley of the shadow of death,
i will fear no evil . . . for Thou art with me. Thy rod and
Thy staff, they comfort me. Thou anointest my head with
oil . . . my cup overfloweth . . . surely goodness and mercy
will follow me all the days of my life . . . and i will dwell
in the house of the Lord forever. . . ."

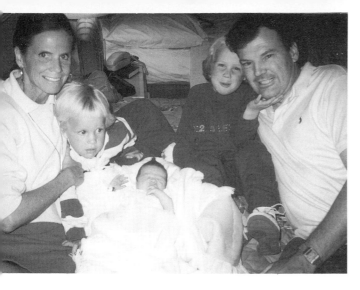

Taking twenty-four hour old Brandt home from the hospital.

I ♥ Louv you ♥
AnNANDBrtó"

(Kindergarten) ffom Tbuyint

"Can we really keep him mommy?" asked Colson.

We all love to read.

Taylor Anderson
December 4, 1990
I Love mom from Taylor
I Love DaD
I Love Brockso to mom And dad I Love
I Love colson every
I Love BranDt Body
in my family

Do you remember what it is like to take a family picture?

Colson's
first birthday.

I love to climb Colson's bunkbed.

Brock and Taylor, best friends.

Stairs up to the children's world.

I oLouvi you

WiLL Anbohos

from Taylor

(Kindergarten)

Brock is a flower boy in a wedding, (1990).

he began to take deep, heaving breaths . . . gasping . . . and boarded his chariot for the Celestial City. we stood in reverent awe, and wept. and knew how rich Heaven would now be with his sweet, gentle presence.

"daddy, what do you want to do when you get to Heaven?" we had asked him only hours before.

"i would like to stand at the Gate and welcome everyone as they come through."

today, at the Gates of Heaven, a little bald-headed-with-white-wisps man stands. if you meet him there before i do, please tell him i am coming, too. through the grace of Jesus. for only Jesus can help me face my mountains. fight my battles. try to be pure and loving in such an impure, loveless world.

my brother landed in hawaii almost the very moment my father died. my father passed him in the skies.

at the funeral, before the service, an elegant little white-haired woman approached us in the church (honolulu first nazarene). we had grown up there. been nurtured in our faith. my dad had prayed and preached there, and loved and forgiven through the primed years of his ministry.

"excuse me," she spoke, "are you the family of the reverend kiemel?"

"yes . . . " we responded.

"i hope you will forgive me for being so bold as to come today, not knowing your father. all my life, i have searched for truth. i have been to the honolulu library, and borrowed every single book on the subject of prayer, and read each one. when i read your father's obituary, in the newspaper, i was overwhelmed. i knew he had to be a holy man. somehow, i just had to come and see what a holy man really looks like."

tears began to stream down our faces.

"the whole world has gone mad," she continued, "i have longed for sterling Christianity! it is such an honor to be here. your father possessed it. oh, thank you for just allowing me to have a glimpse of a holy man."

in life . . . and even death . . . harold kiemel glorified Jesus.

one of the hardest days of my life was watching the big, black, limousine pull into my parents' driveway. saying my last good-byes to my father that somehow i thought would live forever.

he was buried in hawaii. the land he most loved. the dream he had always carried. among orientals. the people he most LOVED, on his tombstone we printed the simple, but profound, motto of his entire life . . .

"IT PAYS TO SERVE JESUS"

daddy, i miss you.
i miss your prayers.
i long to pass your heritage on to my children and to all ever placed in my path.

> the service of Jesus true pleasure affords . . .
> in Him there is joy. without an alloy.

tis' heaven to trust Him, and rest on His Word . . .
it pays to serve Jesus each day.

it pays to serve Jesus. it pays every day . . .
it pays every step of the way . . .
though the pathway to glory may sometimes be
     dreary . . .
you'll be happy each step of the way.

10. ann—motherhood

mothers really have their own secret club. hearts that understand each other. common threads that bind us together
in love . . . moments of desperation . . . longing to be truly
whole for our children. there is a place, in most mothers'
hearts, that seeks to protect children from harm and evil
and unfairness. for most women, mothers or not, it is as
natural as breathing and sleeping.

no matter how we fail . . . how far short our reach, deep in
our hearts i believe is a softness and love and compassion
that leaves most men trying to pull us back to the center.
not understanding how sincere (even if sincerely wrong)
our motives are.

this is potty training time for my two youngest sons. i
major in boys. little girls are sort of a mystery to me
though i once was one.

"mommy, you watch, okay?" colson pleads.

"okay, sweetheart. you go on into the bathroom. i am
coming."

brandt comes in and crawls on my lap as i sit on the floor
in front of colson on the toilet.

taylor sticks his head in, "if you make a mess, colson,
mommy will give you a treat!"

colson looks up with a terrible frown on his face. as if to say, "you stay out of this!"

brandt starts grunting to inspire colson. brock brings the candy basket in when he hears us clapping and shrieking. rewards go a long way with my children in potty training. but more, habit. ritual. a system helps. every time i change a diaper, i head them for the potty.

nothing terrifies me as much as potty training. honestly, i did not think i could accomplish it. somehow, it seemed over my head. the world is full, however, of adults who all went to the bathroom, and i found comfort in that daily. it buoyed my spirits every time i had this trembling thought that my child would go to first grade in diapers. maybe even junior high. surely, they all learned somehow?

I cannot tell you how many times i have been squirted in the face while i sat on the floor in front of the toilet, trying to cheer my little boys on. nor how many times i wiped up drips all over the bathroom floors.

colson has just learned how to stand on his tiptoes just enough to go potty like the big boys.

toothbrushes are another problem. all four of my sons, as toddlers, have been addicted to toothpaste. will, more than i, has worried about so much floride in their systems. i finally gave up when they continued to look so healthy, and the dentist keeps telling me how good all their teeth are.

during teething, taylor through brandt have loved chewing and gnawing on a toothbrush. having a clean, relatively new toothbrush used to be a big thing to me. after catching the children using the toilet water to brush their teeth, i became radical about it. i would keep running their toothbrushes through the dishwasher, but even that made my stomach queasy.

however, when i have an appointment, and cannot find a toothbrush anywhere, i have definitely lowered my standards. under the bed . . . in an already stuffed drawer . . . by the kitchen counter, on the floor . . . i swish whatever i can find, recklessly, under hot water, and start brushing. blocking, as much as i can, my rampant imagination on where it might have been an hour earlier.

will and i flew in from seattle one evening. tiffany and the little boys were at the gate.

"colson go on the plane!" cried colson.

"yes, darling," i kissed him, lifting him in my already crowded arms. "next time."

we decided to stop at a pizza place next to a large albertson's supermarket . . . maybe ten yards from the side door. everyone indulged in smorgasbord pizza, all you could eat. brock and taylor were in heaven when two very nice off-duty policemen came in for dinner in their full uniforms and helped dish a third helping of pizza onto their plates.

i suddenly looked around.

"where is colson?" i asked trying to be calm.

will was walking back to the table from the far side of the pizza parlor. "colson has disappeared! i can't find him anywhere."

everyone was mystified. in just a seeming instant, he had gone. his little towhead was nowhere to be found.

frantically turning our heads one way, and then another, we searched, almost in slow motion, riveted in horror to our seats.

will found him outside, halfway to the pizza restaurant door dragging a huge box of ladies' sanitary napkins behind him. he was yelling, "daddy, diapers! i got diapers." the albertson clerk was running through the dark, cold outdoors after him.

"is anyone shopping with this child?" he asked.

will and i did not want to claim him as he'd stolen, innocently, that giant box of modess. terribly embarrassed, will handed the box back to the store clerk, apologizing profusely, while all the pizza eaters looked on. i grabbed all their coats, tiffany helping, and we left quickly.

on the way out, will thanked the policemen for being so nice to the boys as i hurried them out to the car.

taylor and brock, in our former neighborhood, developed a great liking to some neighbors several houses down the block. the neighbors next door . . . our good friends . . . laughed and related what the man next door to them had said.

he and his wife would chat with taylor and brock while on their tricycles. brock looked at the man and asked,

"are you a stranger?" the man replied, "no. i'm a neighbor."

brock's comeback was, "oh, that's good! because we are not supposed to talk to strangers."

it reminds me of when jan and i were small. my parents were always challenging us to have good manners in "public." a lady took us to the waldorf astoria for dinner, and jan looked up, speaking loudly,

"is this what you call the 'public'?"

my mother used to tell us that she never enjoyed eating out while we were small. it always rather offended me. now i understand! one of my favorite pleasures is eating quietly with will or other adults, while the children are in somebody's kitchen being tended. i do not prefer being on display in a restaurant with four toddlers!

one afternoon, i treated the little boys to baskin-robbins ice cream cones. strapping them back in their car seats, cones in hand, i slowly drove down seventeenth street for home.

suddenly, i heard brandt trying to scream, with only a muffled, awful sound coming out. looking in my rearview mirror, i had to quickly pull the car over before crashing it. each child was in his own world, licking away at his cone, except brandt.

brandt's cone was somehow stuck in his mouth and his nose at the same time, just sticking there, while he waved his hands wildly, not knowing how to pull it off.

how could anyone intentionally scar a child's heart and mind? sure, when colson and brandt break a dozen eggs on the kitchen floor when i run to grab the phone, i can get close to sort of losing it. or the day the house got quiet in

an instant, and i could not find the babies or hear them or
see them. some friends had picked brock and taylor up for
a little circus in town, but it was way too quiet for the babies to not be in some sort of trouble.

looking out the entry window, i saw these barely two-year-
olds, hand-in-hand, varied boots on their feet, walking down
the middle of the road. genuinely trying not to slip on my
face, i flew out the double front doors . . . the circle drive . . .
the large, front yard . . . down the road . . . to them.

colson's eyes were flashing with determination. brandt was
only an innocent bystander, dragged along by his brother.
"i go to the circus, too!' colson forged ahead.

late at night, i crawl into bed, and often shudder. what if
children did not have angels? what if God's love did not
trace them? what if no romans 8:28 existed? "all things
working together for good?"

adolescence terrifies me. our children will be pushing us
around in a wheelchair. toddlers surely are easier. sometimes!

"Jesus, please make us your instruments for these children.
the world out there is so sick and mean and calloused and
dangerous. our children seem so small and exposed.

protect them, Lord . . . please . . . and may we always remind them, as they grow, that they are sinners needing
grace. may they never grow up sinning and non-repentant.
may we be their humble leaders in confession and the embracing of your power, hourly.

amen.
amen. amen.

෴ ෴ ෴

I will sing to my child, I will dream
    with my son.
I will hold him and rock him and show
    him my love.
We will laugh, we will play, we will dance
    through the day. . . .
with a prayer in our hearts for the world
    God has made.

            (Merilee Zdnek)

11. we stand for life

will and i are definitely pro-life. in every situation. we do
want to be careful not to become as angry about abortion
as the pro-choice people are toward us. we feel anger does
not accomplish much. creative options for girls are much
more productive.

one day, mary, a dear friend who works with the local
pregnancy hot line, called. she had just done a pregnancy
test on a girl. it was positive. the girl had given up a baby
for adoption at fourteen, had a second son a few years
later, marrying the birthfather and then having to leave
him because of abuse.

this was her third pregnancy. a new father whom she
scarcely knew and who had already left town. mary had arranged for her to at least come and talk to me, and she
said, "ann, i feel really special about this girl. she is
adopted herself. she has lived a wild life. she has a beautiful face. i am praying, ann, that she will show up for her
appointment."

right then, i started praying aloud with mary. my heart felt
stirred, too. the Holy Spirit seemed to convict me of the spe-
cialness of this situation.

"ann, really pray for this girl. she has to be about six
months pregnant, and has an appointment in salt lake, next
week, to have an abortion," added mary.

the next day, i visited at my office, and marybeth never
showed. i felt heartsick. she had refused to leave her last
name or phone number with mary, and we were helpless
in trying to locate her.

hourly, i prayed for the Lord to intervene. to SOMEHOW
keep marybeth from the abortion.

a couple days later, i received a call from a baptist church
in town. they had spoken with a woman in their church
whose daughter was pregnant. she had called for counsel
and advice, knowing her daughter was planning to abort,
and not feeling right about her grandbaby being killed at
close to seven months of development. could they send this
mother to me for counsel?

of course, i agreed willingly to talk. as i put the phone re-
ceiver down, it clicked in me that maybe this was the same
girl that had not showed earlier in the week.

the mother was lovely. warm. genuine. feeling desperate for
she had done much of the care for her two-year-old grand-
child that her daughter already had. she could not see taking
on another baby, nor could she stand the thought of abortion. i suggested i come to their house to talk to the daughter. to make sure an appointment was kept.

this is a miracle story. it was the same girl. she had decided
to go ahead with the abortion and not come in to see me.
God then had personally placed her mother in my life. this
was a scared, special life, and God absolutely intervened,
beyond human control, to spare it.

this birthmother sat at her mother's kitchen table. beautiful,
olive skin, and eyes. she confessed to being a terrible rebel.

she shared her fears about giving this baby up. she was adopted and had never really resolved that herself. and what if it was a little girl? what she had always wanted. she could not do that!

following that first encounter, i spent many hours on the phone and in person with marybeth. she had been willing to cancel the abortion. it was my job, with God's help, to guide marybeth into a decision she could live with . . . and one i prayed that was best for the baby.

in the south, a couple had driven several hours from visiting their parents' homes to where they lived. they had read my book, *open adoption*, and felt deeply that they wished they could connect with me. however, it seemed impossible.

rick and cammie were at a professional basketball game with one of rick's friends, who had a darling date he wanted them to meet. rick mentioned to his friend about their spiritual encounter, reading my book. the friend's eyes sparkled, for his date was one of will's and my own birthmothers. the mother of one of our little boys.

cammie and my birthmother had been in the bathroom. when they came out, rick's friend suggested our birthmother tell her story, he knew she had had a baby. given it up for adoption. was proud of her courage, and supportive of her sharing it as testimony to God's grace.

as our birthmother began her story, rick and cammie were electrified by the miracle. she knew me? i was the adoptive mother to her baby? could she connect them to us?

aren't God's plans amazing! intricately interwoven with
sterling nuggets of wonder. only Jesus could have put such
an encounter together.

rick and cammie called my office the day after i had first
met with marybeth. though i had never personally met
them, i utterly trusted my birthmother's evaluation of
them. everything seemed knitted in transcendant design. i
felt they were the adoptive couple if marybeth did decide
to release.

today, rick and cammie have a beautiful baby girl.
marybeth went to their city to deliver. they witnessed the
birth. though it was a baby girl, marybeth had surrendered
her life to the Lord with the lovely family who kept her.
who followed God's call. she obeyed. surrendered. for the
first time in her life, marybeth did something truly selfless.
she was empowered by a giant God.

she now lives in the northwest, working. going to alcohol-
ics anonymous. living with a strong Christian family. being
nurtured and discipled by kathy, a radiant believer.
marybeth is truly trying in God's power, to turn her life
around.

a baby girl, three months old now . . . bright-eyed and
happy and beautiful . . . is alive! her little life was not de-
stroyed by the brutal act of abortion. the world is going to
be changed by that one, small child. rick and cammie are
radiant, grateful parents.

today, as i write this, rick and cammie have flown in to
show the baby to marybeth's family. just so she will not be
a mystery to them in all the years to come. marybeth has
come on a bus . . . many hours . . . to celebrate the week-

end with them. to have one more peek at the baby she was brave enough to carry, deliver, and relinquish.

a miracle. God lives for miracles. watch. you'll see!

another experience that totally convinced me that life is absolutely sacred . . . that abortion is utterly wrong . . . comes from a family in iowa. the pregnant girl's mother had written me, and called me by phone, for years . . . though we had never met face-to-face. janet was a single mom. two daughters. katie, the oldest, was somewhat mentally handicapped and impregnated by a boy next door. her mother had become desperate, unable to really guide and control katie. finally, with anguish, she turned her over as a ward of the state.

loving my books, janet called and asked if i could talk to katie by phone.

the state of iowa had never allowed a girl they were in charge of to go out-of-state to deliver a baby. Katie had such a hard time considering the possibility of giving up the baby. the social workers did not want her mother to make the decision for her, and janet was very wise and tried to stand back.

many moments . . . numerous phone calls and letters . . . left me feeling a sense of hopelessness for this situation. katie was not capable of raising a baby. if she did give it up, she wanted to come to idaho and have me help her, she and her mom really wanted to know where the baby would go.

one day, i received a letter from janet, and a picture of katie. when, miraculously, katie did come to idaho, i fell in love with her. gentle. sweet. so simplistic in her faith and trust. she took one day at a time. her mind was not complex enough to worry about all the days ahead.

my secretary at the time was a great Christian human being. she and her husband had prayed fifteen years for a baby. finally, after much infertility and surgery, she had a hysterectomy. several adoptions had fallen through. everything seemed hopeless.

i walked over to her desk the friday the picture came.

"pam, this would be a miracle. all the legalities and pieces look impossible. but what do you think about the girl in this picture who is pregnant?

pam knew all the specifics about katie. she held the picture a moment, and looked up with tears in her eyes.

"ann, i see potential in her. great potential!"

"pam, you are the mother for this baby! if God puts it together, your heart is perfect to receive this little life!"

i had a conference call with the social workers in iowa. katie and janet and i talked. katie said she had decided to release the baby, but she wanted to come here, and have me handle the adoption.

the state of iowa gave katie twenty days in idaho to come, deliver, and return to her home state. even twenty days was a miracle. now, if God could just help us to get her delivered in time!

there were still doubts in my mind. would katie really be able to give this baby up? it represented someone to love her. a girl's mother plays such an important role in an adoption process. if she does not support her daughter's decision to release the baby, then i have grave doubts about getting involved. janet was totally behind the adoption, and i knew she would have a key impact.

everyone who works with me fell in love with katie and her mom. pam and dale got along beautifully with them. about a week from the twentieth day, katie went into labor. would the baby be healthy? would everything be okay? somehow, deep within me, i had blind faith in God's sovereign goodness and love. whatever.

jim, my ob-gyn, decided with me that we should do a caesarean. katie was panicking over the intense pain. i went into the surgery room, and held katie's hand while my anesthetist friend, eileen, put her out. pam stood on the other side of the window, where they hand the baby through to be checked. she had a better view than i did. it was the first c-section for me to witness.

the most beautiful, perfect, alert baby boy was born in a moment i will never forget. not a flaw. an extra-special baby. a touch of red in his hair.

katie amazed us all. so brave. so serene. so sweet. so steadfast in her decision. her mother, janet, was likewise amazing. i really believe it is harder on the girl's mother than anyone. her grandchild. watching her daughter grieve through such an act of love . . . and loss.

pam, at forty, was handed joshua, one of the greatest desires of her heart. she and dale act as if they have had five.
so relaxed. so wonderful with this charming child.

they waited.
God answered.
in His time
through a most incredible situation.
Jesus honored pam and dale
for their love for katie, and their trust in God's sovereignty.

some of the most beautiful gifts come from unexpected
packages. thanks, great God. thanks, iowa!

this letter is from one of the birthmoms from new hope. it
so expresses the struggles and the obedience—

Dear Ann,

Thursday morning when we left the hotel, I was so excited to get
home. When we drove in the driveway, it seemed like I had been
gone for a year instead of a month.

You know something, Ann, it seems like I don't even know people here since I've been back. I went to a school dance for a little
while on Friday and I felt so strange and like a foreigner! I
couldn't wait to leave! The kids at the dance were all from my
class, (it was a dance for us seniors only), and they knew me. But
when they saw me, a lot of them, actually all of them except
about seven, looked at me like I had some kind of disease or
something. I mean, they weren't the people I had usually associ-
ated with, but when I was pregnant and they knew, they never
looked at me as they did this past Friday. I can already see that
going back to school in January is going to be a challenging task.

Today after church I talked to my baby's birthfather. At first I was scared and uncomfortable but after a bit I began to relax. I showed him all the pictures and I could see the tears in his eyes. His mom cried when she saw the pictures. But she knew that the right decision was made. Bob and I talked more after everyone left. I told him about Kevin and Joanie and shared about your work with open adoption. He seemed at ease, but he told me that the only reason he signed the release papers (for Margaret's adoption) was because I begged him to do so before I flew to Idaho. Silently, after Bob said that, I just praised God for His hand in this whole thing.

Ann, I want you to know that without you I could never have done what I did. If I wouldn't have come to Idaho, little Margaret may not be where she is today—in a loving Christian home with not only one, but two wonderful parents. Thank you so much from the bottom of my heart! Hopefully, one day down the road you will be able to meet Margaret when she is older (maybe around my age). I think it is important for her to get the opportunity one day to meet you. Too, one day, I hope to sit down with Margaret and tell her why I did what I did.
That will be my forever dream—to sit and talk with her face to face. But for right now all I can do is wait and hope for that day to arrive.

Ann, my mom was right when she said that leaving that great support system in Idaho was going to be hard. Since I've come home it feels as if the break in my heart has gotten a lot bigger. Also, being farther from Kevin and Joanie and Margaret is harder. As I told my mom after I first got home, I so wish that I had little Margaret here at home with me. But then I was pushed back to reality and told myself that she is better off with Kevin and Joanie. Someday though, I'll have another baby. Right!

Well, Ann, I will close for now. You're a great and wonderful person, Ann. I wish there were more people like you in my life. Thank you so much for everything you've done for me in the past few months. I will never be able to repay you! Keep in touch!

> Love forever in
> Christ,
>
> Christy

P.S. Have you gotten your book finished? Good luck with it! You're in my thoughts and prayers.

> ". . . Friends are friends forever
> if the Lord's the Lord of them. . . ."

12. *jackson hole*

it was Christmas time. 1989. will had business in jackson hole, wyoming. he always loves for us to go along. with a two-hour drive each way, and not knowing how long it might take, we left the babies with a wonderful family, and headed out with taylor and brock.

there was snow everywhere. skiers on the slopes. people from all over the world. shoppers. will headed to the hospital to meet with doctors about a new device he had discovered, and the boys and i headed off to browse, eat ice cream cones, warm ourselves by the big, roaring fire in the city's old hotel. will promised to meet us in that lobby in three hours.

every shop was bustling with people. i had forgotten to put ski hats in for the boys. being so cold, we went into every shop to keep warm. to buy the boys hats. to sip soup before ice cream.

in every store, someone from some part of the country came up.

"aren't you ann kiemel?"

everyone was so warm, so friendly. so special. i smiled. i tried to be very warm and kind, for they all were.

taylor and brock yanked on my coat. when i introduced them to new people, they became shy. lowered their eyes. pleaded to move on.

i was embarrassed! where were their manners? why were they not looking into the eyes of these people . . . answering in more audible voices.

at the corner drug, we sat on stools at the old-fashioned counter. first, my children could not decide which kind of ice cream they wanted. then they wanted what the other one had. then brock's scoop fell onto the floor, and he started wailing.

suddenly, a darling college student sat down and said, "aren't you ann kiemel?"

i was horrified. we had disrupted the entire store. i was not looking like the perfect mother.

"ann, i heard you speak a few years ago, and i have read most of your books. are these your children?"

i tried very hard to get my children to respond. to smile. to quiet down. i wiped ice cream off their faces. still smiling, told them to lower their voices. taylor started asking me to buy him some little gadget he saw from the shelf. i chatted with this girl, and tried to act like a very normal and capable mother.

brock fell off his stool. we had to get another ice cream cone for him. again, i tried to quiet him. to smooth his and taylor's hair, rumpled from ski hats.

i finally paid the waitress. left an extra tip for all the disruption. hugged the darling college girl good-bye. taking each of the boy's hands, i left the drug store.

as we clung to each other's hands, walking fast to the next store, i started in, "taylor and brock, mommy is humiliated. all these friendly people. everyone wanting to meet the two little boys they have read about in mommy's books, and you are embarrassing me terribly. if you do not start smiling, and looking people in the eye when they speak to you, and saying 'yes' and 'no' and 'thank you'. . . well, i am going to tell your father. there is no place here i can really spank you, but you KNOW what daddy will do if he hears you are not obeying me!"

they seemed to hear. to take notice. immediately, in the next store, a very attractive, warm couple from colorado walked up with their sons. taylor and brock were much more attentive, responsive.

when we walked out, taylor said,

"mommy, were we sweet enough? Did we smile enough?"

"mom," brock looked up, "would daddy be pleased? are you going to tell him how nice we were?"

how do single moms make it? where does their support come from? homes without strong father figures?

i missed will at the hotel lobby. i finally walked the little boys down the street to a juicy, old-fashioned hamburger place.

we shared french fries, and giant hamburgers that dripped
with mustard, with pickles falling out. we shared a chocolate milkshake, old-fashioned style. we laughed and talked.
i kissed them. we told funny stories. the little boys' legs
swung from the stools.

wandering back to the hotel lobby, we sat by the warm
fire, and watched people. where was will anderson?

finally, i walked over to the front desk in the lobby, and
said, "has will anderson left a message for anyone?" (he
had been looking for me, but couldn't find me and went
back to the hospital.)

"will—no—but you look terribly familiar," smiled the hotel
clerk. "aren't you ann kiemel?"

i smiled shyly. we were all worn out. frazzled.

"yes," i replied, quietly desperate. "are there any taxi-cabs
to the hospital?"

"no, but i will be off work in five minutes, and i would
love to drive you and the boys over," she responded. what
a kind lady!

at 9:30 p.m., we dragged into the hospital emergency area,
and stayed in the visiting room while i had will paged. he
came bounding out. hugged us each warmly. explained he
couldn't find us, and went to bring the car around.

the boys and i rushed out, and started crawling in. will
started to drive off before i got my door closed.

"honey, you must *never* do that again! the little boys take time to get in, and you will leave one of them if you aren't careful." i reprimanded.

"i am sorry, ann, but i did not realize you were not in," will replied, squeezing my hand.

"honey, i mean it . . ."

"mommy," taylor pulled my collar from the back seat. "mommy!"

"taylor, do *not* interrupt mommy. i am talking to daddy . . . will, please, honey, you MUST BE MORE CAREFUL!"

"mommy . . ."

"taylor! what did i just say?"

"mommy, brock got left back there. he did not get in in time," taylor pleaded.

will instantly braked the car. it was dark and very cold, with snow coming up on either side from the hospital.

looking in the rearview mirror, with the brake lights lighting up the back of the car, he could see little brock running as fast as he could toward the car. screaming. crying.

"will!" i screamed, "we left brock!"

"mommy, i was trying to tell you," wailed taylor.

i flew out the door, and ran toward my little four year old
brock. scooping him in my arms, will met me, and we carried him to the car, all of us in tears. our brown-eyed,
sweet-natured, beautiful, second-born.

"darling, are you okay?" i pleaded.

"un-huh," he sobbed, "but i was trying to get in the car
and it just left me!"

i fastened brock into his seat belt, and tried to calm myself,
and him, too. will could not help but laugh, since i had
commanded taylor to be QUIET while he kept trying to tell
us, and i was too busy lecturing will.

for miles, will began to ask the little boys "what if" questions which is one of our family games.

"what if we really had left you out there, brock, without
knowing? what would you have done?"

"well, i would climb up one of those trees so a bear could
not get me," sniffed brock.

questions to make both the boys think. quiet, grateful
hearts for two little boys that belong to us, as gifts from
God. and who ultimately belong to God Himself, but made
us a family. two babies at home, tucked into cribs, and a
Christmas tree that we all decorated together.

for years i thought i would NEVER be a mother. that the
road would NEVER turn a corner. yes, my childhood
dream of motherhood had to die before God could resur-
rect it in a far more powerful way than i had ever imagined.

in God's time, sunrises come. new humiliations even out of those sunrises. but God's love covering it all . . . and all our children accounted for.

13. grandmother's one hundredth birthday party

four little boys were stuffed side-by-side in the back seat. a baby in the carseat on each side, and taylor and brock, barely five and six, in seatbelts in the middle. brock's job always is to be responsible for brandt, our littlest, seated beside him. taylor cares for colson, two-and-a-half, on the other side. if either baby yells, we generally know one or the other boys has probably made a face at the baby, or done SOMETHING to aggravate him. will tries to keep his eye on them in the rear view mirror up front.

they were all screaming and fussing, and i, up front, could not seem to keep the group in order. will swerved off the highway, and sternly said,

"you drive, ann—i will take care of the back seat . . ."

i was rather put out . . . more at will than even the kids. he expected me to command order and silence without completely pulling off the road and spanking them. of course, as soon as will was in my side, and we pulled back onto the freeway, they did quiet down. a six-foot two-and-a-half inch man with a deep male voice does instill more fear . . . or respect.

i felt tired and completely irritated. we had had a wonderful family trip to portland, oregon, to attend will's

131

grandmother's one hundredth birthday. it had been unforgettable . . . an anderson family reunion, with cookouts and
balloons and a spectacular party.

we had, all six, been squeezed into two hotel rooms that
ranked about C+, with two cribs, little shoes strewn everywhere, dirty clothes in a pile, and i tried to keep us all looking fresh and crisp and smiling and united in the midst of
all that.

will's remarkable grandmother has a master's degree . . .
read books in latin from faraway libraries until her nineties
. . . and had profoundly taught and shaped all the
grandchildren's lives. she had three sons: will's dad, with a
law degree and one of the world's largest seed potato
ranches when he died. another who was an orthopedic sur-
geon, married to a psychiatrist. the third, a scientist, who
had a key role with the moon landing.

after the party . . . while i was driving . . .

on the way home . . .

as i drove our air-conditioned, finely tuned car, the engine
began to whine and sputter, the oil gauge dropped, and
there was a terrible noise. i swung to the side of the road
. . . off the shoulder . . . and said,

"will, something terrible is happening to the car!"

the sky was dark, spitting rain, and will crawled out of the
front passenger side and lifted the hood. when i tried to
start the car again, it only made this maddening, clicking
sound, without even a grunt of turning over.

huge trucks were whistling by, and with each one, our car, though heavy like a truck, would shake. i began to hold my breath each moment. i really felt the wind would pick us up and throw us over.

i had mentioned to will months earlier that i had hit a "twig" going down the road by home. just a little stick. he had crawled down and looked under the car, and could see a hole in the oil pan . . . where all the oil had drained out.

"ann," he frowned, "i believe you hit a log! all the oil has drained out through that hole and i am afraid the engine is damaged." he fixed the oil pan and replaced the oil before this trip. but now we were stuck.

at this point i was horrified. we were forty miles from boise, where a mercedes dealership was . . . out in the middle of nowhere. our finances had been pretty tight lately, and will had even packed peanut butter and jelly, bananas, milk and ice water for lunches along the way. no fun at all in my mind, and now a blown engine. pretty grim.

grabbing brock from the back seat, will yelled through the wind and the rain that they would cross the hedge highway, and hitchhike back to boise.

"if i have brock, people will trust me more, and be more likely to stop! anyway, i like company," he smiled.

slamming the door, he dragged brock across the massive freeway, and i started to cry. would i ever see my little son again? or my husband? the babies started crying, feeling my pain, and i closed my eyes every time a massive truck would storm by, begging God to spare us.

after two hours of roadside disaster . . . children crying and pushing and fogging up the windows . . . and smelling as if someone needed to use the bathroom . . . a man stopped. i asked him to send a policeman to rescue me. soon, a patrol car pulled up. the policeman loaded us all in the car (the little boys were ECSTATIC . . . a REAL police officer!) he dropped us at a little motel in a small town called mountain home. soon, a wonderful friend, bob arrived . . . will had called him. he had a little volkswagen, with no roof. the rain had cleared . . . we all crawled in, and as i chewed my hair that outrageously blew, i prayed God would give me joy and submission to His plan. i had already waited two hours by the side of the road, with three little boys.

bob and sheila had a little guest house with no furniture, but a bath . . . and clean and carpeted. we dragged the children and bags and bottles and other paraphernalia in.

the first night was wonderful. baby sitters came, and bob and shiela and will and i had a QUIET, relaxed dinner at a japanese restaurant, with ice cream at baskin-robbins afterward.

only a week before, i had cried and told will i wanted to be more submissive, more pliable. for will, he desired a more consistent schedule. laying all their clothes out the night before. dinner at 5 p.m. quality time with the children. the baby going down at 7 p.m. the others at 7:45 p.m. to 8 p.m. i was trying to live in this quiet, mellow role. the perfect wife and mother. i just hadn't planned on the engine blowing out on the freeway, and all of us sprawled out in a little, contained space again.

the second morning, brandt threw up all over his mattress, the sheets, himself. the kind of mess only a mother can

cleanup without being stricken herself. will was gone for
hours at a time, wildly searching for a car after discovering
a replacement engine for our car would cost four thousand
dollars and would have to be ordered.

i vacuumed. i read stories. we rented videos. i created fun
in the back yard with four rather exhausted, dislocated children. all the time, will would come in and go out quickly
with another horror story about some car he was thinking
of buying to get us home.

when one decides to submit more as a spiritual, earnest person, it feels like such a glorious challenge.

i was inspired and dedicated until this happened.

all my childhood pain around the massive, old "carryall"
my preacher-dad drove all started coming back to me. my
sister and i crawled under the dash, on the floor, praying
no one from school would see us. our joyful willingness to
be dropped off from school two-to-three blocks away, and
walking all the rest of the distance. peeking out the door a
second to make sure no one was remotely close. then plung-
ing out and never looking back.

my little girl fears welled up in me. what if will did something crazy, like buying a "carryall"? we were good friends
with larry burkett, a well known Christian financial plan-
ner. only recently, we had met him in a hyatt hotel in at-
lanta and had done a radio program with him. the potato
farmer, with the largest seed potato ranch in the world,
having to auction off all his farm equipment and start over.
it was a great story on the air. especially since the crisis
had passed.

i know will would love to test my humble commitment to submission. how could he understand? his family had owned and driven numerous mercedes. he even had driven a corvette.

"oh Jesus, i never thought you would throw this at me!" i wailed.

suddenly, i began throwing up. i ached all over. i spent every five minutes on my knees in front of the toilet in this little bathroom, with all four little boys hanging over me. pulling on my shirt, asking over and over,

"mommy, you sick? huh, mommy?"

then i would stumble back to the mattress on the floor where we were sleeping.

finally, will came home, and there i was . . . draped across the mattress. white. hollow-eyed. feverish. my one sick baby limp beside me. a video going for the other three so i could lie down . . . watch them . . . throw up . . . and not lose track of their safety.

will picked me up and hauled me out to a "great car i know you will like, honey. . . . it's in mint condition."

i was horrified as he settled me in the front seat of a 1976 nova. some horrible brown paper stuffed in the air-conditioning vent.

"i'm taking you and brandt to the emergency room, and this will give you a chance to test the car with me!"

i was in shock, but too sick to make much noise. besides being a dirty brown car, i do not remember much else about it except it had a rattle, and i hated it.

taylor, six, crawled in and said, "mommy, this car doesn't have electric windows!"

"i know, darling," i smiled. that was the least of my worries.

"lots of cars don't have electric windows."

i laid my head back, as we drove to the emergency room, tears rolling down my face.

"honey," will chuckled, "this is a chance to praise the Lord. remember the verse, 'rejoice always!'"

i did not like will anderson at that moment. i thought life, that had only hours earlier been exciting, now completely disappointing. and submission? i would NEVER get so carried away again!

the little boys, except for brandt, were chirping and laughing and reassuring their dad they LOVED the new car! how could they?

the doctor was so kind and caring. "you were very dehydrated and hot. i will make you feel better."

he gave me a shot for pain and nausea, and prescriptions for the baby and me. waiting in a parking lot of a pharmacy, while will went in to get prescriptions filled, i found myself sliding down low.

oh, Jesus, my whole identity is messed up in this car. i feel
as if i am eight again.

no pain shot could numb the awful realization that will anderson just might buy this to get us home in. and maybe he
would enjoy the humble lifestyle so much that we would
never even see a 1980s car again!

the next day, he bounded into our small guest quarters.
all smiles.

"let's pack up, honey. i passed on the nova because the air-
conditioning didn't work. i have bought a car that i think
you *will* like better, and it only cost $650. while they are fix-
ing the mercedes, it will be our wheels, and i bet i can sell
it in idaho falls for a profit!"

with trembling heart, i peeked out the door. my tears
started again. there sat a maroon, 1975 dodge dart.

"ann, you are acting like a snob!"

"i know, honey, but you did not grow up feeling so poor
and rejected. this is a terrible shock since we have driven a
mercedes our whole married life. a '75 dodge dart is such a
gaping distance from what i have gotten used to. and we
will probably drive it FOREVER!"

i started sobbing again, and all four little boys were
quiet . . . but seemingly as happy and relaxed as can be!

❧ ❧ ❧

it has been seven weeks, and today a young couple is picking up the dart, to drive to kansas. they saw the ad in the

paper. we did sell it for a profit . . . it did get us around
without causing problems . . . will is out looking at another
car because the engine is just now being put into the mercedes, and we need something we can fit into. we hope, really, to sell the mercedes and buy a new van. there are too
many of us to fit into much else. especially if our family
were to enlarge at all.

until the mercedes is fixed, will has his eye on a '73 lincoln
continental. it makes the dart look good.

today, i really would not change this adventure. i have decided my value is not wrapped up in a car. that i must
grow beyond my childhood pain. that this plan did save us
some money. that i so want my children to be resilient, and
they have been.

but we really are not treated the same. they no longer smile
and call me "Mrs. Anderson" when i drop off my dry cleaning. on saturday mornings when we once in a while pile in
and go to a few garage sales . . . a great treat for the boys
. . . will says, "we are training them to be good bargainers"
. . . it is rather humorous. pouring out of the mercedes, we
were treated with great dignity, but no one would budge
on the prices. now as little boys keep falling out of the dart,
and tiffany, the darling girl who lives with us and helps,
comes along, we appear to be a large family, struggling.

my little boys run and find every little toy for a nickel and
sadly beg for us to buy it. whatever the price, we usually
counteroffer; they almost immediately agree to the lower
price. taylor did get some almost-new saddle oxfords for a
quarter the other day.

i love everyone who drives old cars in a new way now. i really understand what it feels like on the other side. even yesterday, a man looked out of the window of his small business where i was picking up an item.

"that your dodge dart?" he asked.

"yes," i quietly responded.

"about a '74?"

"uh-huh. how did you know? would you like to buy it?"

wouldn't that be wonderful, i thought!

"listen," the man replied, "if you want to sell it, try the trophy shop down the road. that may be an antique, and you could get some money for it!"

happy, healthy children. a warm, sprawling house with lots of room. people to call my friends. new health and vitality. a man with a strong enough ego to be content with anything. living out-of-debt.

i rejoice! i will even kind of miss the dodge dart. not very much, yet a whole lot if will gets the gold continental!

note: will bought a 1982 buick that looks almost new! . . . he is so happy with the "deal" . . . he paid $1950 for this one . . . it is luxury compared to the dart . . . the mercedes will be here tomorrow . . . we also have two vans to choose from . . .

i ask will to forgive me . . . will i ever learn to trust my husband? . . . trust God? God keeps loving me by giving me opportunities . . . to trust my First Love . . . i keep missing it.

14. saturday family shopping

we must get our lives together. that was how will was feeling. not enough structure. too many loose ends. a more
earnest commitment to the budget.

"ann, i think we could get the shopping done saturday
morning, maybe in as short a time as thirty minutes," will
announced a couple of weeks ago.

this particular saturday, it was spitting snow and drizzle.
gloomy. cozy inside. a perfect morning to sleep a little.

the alarm went off at 6 a.m. will was out of bed, heading
for the shower. taylor and brock always get to sleep with
us on friday nights, so all the noise awakened them. begging for the one morning we have to take it easy, i let them
go in to watch cartoons.

the oatmeal was cooking on the stove. dishes and spoons
set out. will was soon showered and ready, informing the
boys they must be dressed, with shoes and socks on before
any more television could be watched.

tiffany, our nanny . . . like our child . . . expecting a baby in
two months (and planning to marry the handsome
birthfather in the south in boot camp) . . . stumbled, sleepy-
eyed, passed me for her bath.

141

my husband was very ambitious. we would check prices in four or five places. get all our week's groceries. then have time to bowl, a fun family activity.

a couple of months before, on a saturday, we had taken the four little boys to mcdonald's (their favorite) for sausage biscuits, and then bowling. i was not sure i wanted to bowl again. that afternoon, the little boys were ecstatic. we all (except the two babies) had donned bowling shoes and found our balls.

will was reminding taylor and brock how to roll their ball down the lanee when i noticed brandt, our youngest, running in his little hightops, down the next bowling lane toward the pins. i was mortified, i could just see him falling into that pit and being mangled, so i started after him.

NO ONE had ever told me that the bowling lanes are polished to make them extra slick. the faster i ran after brandt, the more delighted he was by the race . . . and the faster he picked up his pace. his shoes had friction. my smooth-soled bowling shoes did not.

suddenly, my feet flew out from under me. i was tossed in the air. i came down flat on my back with a horrible thump. the back of my head hit so hard i did not think i would ever move again. the pain was excruciating. moaning in pain and utterly humiliated in front of everyone.

"honey, are you okay? i looked up from the score sheet just as your feet went up in the air. you need to be really be careful on these slick lanes."

will leaned down to help me up, and i looked at him in disbelief. like, why are you telling me that now?

i could not hide the tears as will helped carry me out. the pain in my back was intense. the children stared in shock. after hours of x-rays in the emergency room, they found multiple contusions, and i was very sore. all because i am a mom and my mother's instinct forgot EVERYTHING but racing to save my loved child from ruin.

a week later, i developed a major kidney infection because of bruising my kidneys in the fall. recovering from that, i slipped on the carpeted stairs in our house bringing the babies down for their naps. the first fall affected the second fall (i do not have a lot of meat on my bones . . . a family trait) and i broke the tenth rib in the right side of my back.

never ever again will i smile when people tell me horror stories about broken ribs. it was the worst pain i had ever experienced in my life, and it takes weeks of recovery. every time will started to hug me, or my children reached up to pat me, or i breathed, it hurt. a lot. a lot. a lot!

so will's idea of another day of bowling left me terribly skeptical. grocery shopping for bargains did not sound like very much fun with four little boys either.

when will gets an idea or plan in his mind, no one can compete with his energy or enthusiam. his vitality and strength and optimism had always been traits i loved about him. living with these traits was not always easy, however.

tiffany had the list of all the things we needed. in every store, we pulled the carts out to put the babies in, and taylor and brock often took their own carts to push.

we started at payless. will had his computer sheet out, listing all kinds of prices he had collected on different items.

he would send tiffany one direction, me another, and he would head toward a third spot in the store.

in every store, we created a scene. a baby yelled. the bigger boys wanted their carts to push . . . then got lost with their carts. we replaced items, exchanged them. finally, we would haul everyone out of the carts and toward the car. babies in their seats, all the rest of us in seat belts. that day, we were driving the '75 dodge dart.

from payless to albertson's. from albertson's to some meat house. on to reed's dairy to check their prices on milk and hamburger. to the wonder bread discount bread shop. fred meyer's for all-natural peanut butter.

it only took tiffany and me one time of watching that peanut machine roll out peanut butter into lumps that looked like something else . . . to discourage our once enthusiastic taste for peanut butter and jelly sandwiches. it was very inexpensive, and for will, PURE. (his father had died of stomach cancer).

(brock went to a house that had some wonderful generic brand of peanut butter that included the impurities and additives, and looked up with his huge brown eyes shining. "i LOVE your peanut butter!" he exclaimed in wonder.)

we finally ended up at waremart, the big discount grocery store, with many generic brands, and everything still unpacked in boxes. bulk kool-aid. bulk banana pudding in a barrel. the grocery list was almost flawless. the items were broken down to what aisle they are on at waremart, the large, much-cheaper, more economic shopping place. i believe in every store someone recognized me, and with each store down the line, the children became more tired and hungrier and noisier and more restless and fussy.

will and i were standing by the meat department, looking over different packages of chicken when a horrendous crash resounded all around us. we looked up in horror to find that brock had been pushing his cart too fast, and casually cast a look in some other direction. before anyone could stop him, he had bashed his cart into twenty or thirty bottles of wine stacked up, and broke all of them.

wine flowed everywhere. broken glass scattered in all directions. the smell was unforgettable. and every shopper in the area froze and let out these terrible gasps.

as will and i looked over, we saw all four of our children in the middle of it, wet and smelling with wine. tiffany's clothes carried quite an aroma the rest of the day. we begged for mercy as they hauled out mops and brooms, and slithered down the closest aisle.

will said, "ann, when i take the boys shopping myself, everything is smooth. we have a buddy system, and no traumas occur!"

"will anderson," i muttered, "it is 2 o'clock in the afternoon. no one has had lunch. the babies have missed their naps. i refuse to be held accountable!"

suddenly, we burst out laughing. it was too impossibly, terribly hopeless to take too seriously. we might have totally tossed in the towel on parenting, and decided to throw away every ounce of good sense we did have.

back home we dragged starving, exhausted children from the car. bags and bags of groceries from multiple stores. we fed the babies. put them down for naps. will began to calculate what we had spent. obviously, we had not saved. somehow ended up spending more. finished out all our reserve for the day. bowling was absolutely out of the question. not even a trailing thought.

as i fell into bed that night, will suggested we might have a little romance.

no man could be more exciting to me than will. in fact, if something were to happen to him, i cannot even imagine remarrying. he is so perfect for me.

but romance? i rolled my eyes, and only a gutteral noise came from my throat. barely breathing, i said, "will, i have NEVER been so stressed out and exhausted in my whole life. there is something wrong with this shopping plan."

he rolled me into his big, strong arms, shaking with laughter. "ann, you were right, this was not a workable plan. honey, from now on we will just go to one store, and see how fast, we can pick everything up there. i even have all the food items listed in order of the rows at waremart in the computer sheet. honey, thank you for letting me make my own mistakes! I love you"

it sounded like a glorious plan. that is, if i could ever face all the shoppers and employees at waremart again!

i fell asleep thanking the Lord that will anderson only had to learn his lesson once . . . usually. that was a lot more than he could say about me!

15. goodbye carmen

for over a year, i have received a phone call from carmen
every week. i knew she would call. no matter what i was
doing, unless a rare exception, i ALWAYS took carmen's call.

though we had never met face to face, we were friends. she
wrote frequently. sent loving, special cards.

she shared her pain.

her struggles.

her joys.

her thoughts.

often she would play me old hymns on a tape recorder,
over the phone, long distance. she lived hundreds of miles
away, but the written page and the phone were our links.

one friday the hymn she had on . . . that she sang along
with . . . was,

>I don't worry about tomorrow—
>I just live from day to day—
>I don't wonder o'er the shadows
>for the skies will turn from gray. . . .

Many things about tomorrow—
I don't seem to understand.
But I know Who holds tomorrow—
and I know Who holds my hand.

carmen had had a terrible relationship with her father. had been abused and rejected. she was married to john, someone who loved her very much, and tried earnestly to stick with her through some very hard times.

bulemia and anorexia were major struggles. my not being a professional counselor made it hard for me to understand everything, but i did love her and accept her unconditionally.

carmen had lost two babies . . . one when her pregnancy was at four or five months. another at six months. her body was not strong enough to carry a child. to give it enough nourishment. this was devastating for her and john, and finally, carmen went into treatment for several weeks. everyone felt she was on the road to recovery.

probably way too quickly . . . trying to make up for past errors . . . she got pregnant again. maybe it was her way of making it right for john.

after seven weeks, they discovered that she was expecting twins. that they were both boys. she and john were elated.

i knew carmen was smart. she was one of the head checkers at a shopko store in her area. that meant she hussled people through her line at a faster, more competent rate than most.

week after week carmen and i would talk about her twins. about john. it was as if she was at a new place in life. excited. expectant. hopeful. she told me week after week that i was her friend. it always made me feel sad, for i was far away. i felt powerless to invest very much into her.

while will and i and the children were in oregon for will's grandmother's one hundredth birthday, i called carmen. she lived in oregon, not far away, and i wondered if someone could bring her to our hotel so we could meet face-to-face. so i could see this pregnant friend. celebrate the unborn life within her. she was only three weeks from delivery. i was thrilled she had carried the babies almost to term.

over and over, carmen told me her big dream . . . to meet me face-to-face. now we could. and she could see my little sons and meet will. some friend was driving her over.

never do i try to encourage people to put their eyes . . . their focus . . . on me. i am human. i am incredibly imperfect. i will fail. over and over. no one . . . not me or anyone . . . should focus our worship and adoration on ANYONE or ANYTHING but Jesus. ALWAYS, He must be our First Love. even for those of us more mature in the faith, that is a challenge. our sinful, human hearts want to reach out and adore something more tangible and visible.

the night before carmen was to come see me in salem, i called her to make sure everything was in order. she was crying. she had gone for her weekly check-up that afternoon, and her doctor could not pick up one of the heartbeats. the physician was also alarmed because he felt the other baby was not large enough to be delivered yet, and he was thinking of hospitalizing her.

my immediate impulse was to feel upset at this doctor. why would he wait until three weeks, pre-delivery, to be concerned about carmen's weight gain? why hadn't he admitted her to the hospital weeks before and kept her on a rigid, adequate diet?

carmen was sobbing. said she would call tomorrow, after the doctor checked her once more. if there still was only one heartbeat, she would have to be hospitalized. i probably could not see her. our schedule was tight, and the hospital was not even close to our return route home. i prayed with her over the phone. in tears myself.

"ann, i have only gained a few pounds through the whole pregnancy. i do not even look that pregnant. ann, i have tried to eat. i really have," carmen continued, weeping.

again, i could not understand the doctor's lack of concern. until now?

calling the next day, i found carmen packing her things for the hospital. weeping uncontrollably. john was on his way home to take her. she was faced with two deaths. the death of her long dream to meet me face-to-face. the death of one of her babies and maybe of the other one.

with all the love i could pour through the phone, i tenderly pulled her heart next to mine. how well i knew the pain of baby loss, though my circumstances were totally different. though not because of an eating disorder, i always felt somehow guilty and responsible for not carrying healthy pregnancies.

we headed home, with the children, on our memorable trek where the engine blew out on the mercedes. brandt and i got the horrible flu bug. the next friday, however, i was in the office and prayed carmen would call. several times, i had tried to reach john . . . to find the name of the hospital to call her . . . all without success.

friday came and went. no calls from carmen. i dropped her a note.

"carmen . . . i have been so worried about you. what is happening? please let me know. i love you very much. i am praying for you."

the next week, every time i tried to call john and carmen's phone, i received a recording.

"we are sorry, but this line has been disconnected."

trying not to panic, yet feeling panic, i dropped another more desperate note to carmen begging her to call collect. a few days later, i received a letter from john, written in tiny, neat script.

Dear Ann . . .

I hope you are not alone when you read this. Carmen lost both the babies. She also passed away last Tuesday, and her service was three days later. Over two hundred friends came. I had no idea so many people loved her.

[My heart almost stopped. Yet I felt it pulsating so fiercely I felt I might stop breathing. Carmen was GONE? forever?]

As you probably can guess, Ann, she took her life. She told me she was just going to take a little drive, to think. I had to identify

her body, and it wasn't a pretty sight. She had put a bullet
through her head. . . .

I feel so lost. I loved her so much. I feel I wasn't a good husband.
I should have done more for her. I know my wife probably told
you things she did not tell me. I knew she had a traumatic childhood. . . .

I got up and talked at the funeral. I fell apart. I said you were
véry important in her life. Much more than you know. She always talked about you. Said she wished she had the strength
you had.

I feel I have a big hole in my heart. Like it will never go away. I
think I did the best I could. It will be tough this holiday (Christmas). We had the nursery ready. I hurt REAL BAD. My world
has shut down. I had no idea she was planning on dying. No
wife. No children. But I do have GOD!

Ann, I have never written this much in my whole life. I need
somebody to listen. You have been an inspiration.

Love, John.

carmen is gone! she is really gone. no more words to be
spoken to her. no longer the sound of her voice in the
phone. could i have been more loving? more patient? more
redemptive? the sadness and pain shakes me even as i
write. i miss her. long for some . . . any . . . fresh opportunity to point her to my First Love. to the Hope. the promises. the mercy. the forgiveness. the grace.

we have invited john to come see us. just to spend some
time with someone. he is hurting so deeply. he feels so
very lost, alone. will and i desire to prepare a table of
God's great love and kindness and redemption before him.

i know God had great mercy for carmen. for anyone who hurts that deeply, and gets so lost in the fog. so lost until death actually sounds sweet to taste. that is all i know.

more than ever, i long for the First Love of my life to penetrate thoroughly. to somehow be a more healing force for Him in my world.

i miss you, carmen. i will always have more dignity and warmth in my life because you so loved me.

to keep one's eyes on his or her First Love . . . the Savior . . . always promises strength and courage to hang on.

may we not allow our hearts to wander away, for life can be so empty and futile without Jesus.

16. *my mom has alzheimer's*

losing my father . . . watching him board the chariot for Heaven . . . was a joyous-and-sorrowful celebration. it closed out 1989 as the most purifying, tried-by-fire year of my life.

being used to a holy father . . . calling him all hours of the day and night . . . no one on earth would ever love me more purely, more unconditionally . . . left me so gratified for having experienced the gift, but with a gaping wound. my father spent countless hours EVERY day, praying for his children and grandchildren.

he walked prayer. breathed prayer. slept prayer. he believed in "praying through." absolutely not letting go until "heaven fell." until the burden lifted from his heart. he wept over others' sorrows. the Spirit of God so loved through him.

oh, daddy, as i write this, i miss you so. do you see me down here? "Jesus, place his mantle on me."

my beautiful mother became more and more disoriented. confused. repeating thoughts and experiences to us over and over. though my father had taken her to a top neurologist in honolulu, he and others could never seem to diagnose her. my mother had been so sharp. she knew she was failing. my father, in love and respect, never talked about it. not even with us, his children.

six weeks after my father's death, in cleveland with jan . . .
after numerous tests by a geriatric specialist . . . she was
given an evaluation stamped alzheimer's.

even before the diagnosis, we knew we had, in a sense, lost
my mother, too.

though in midlife, it was very, very painful for me. and
continues to be. no one . . . absolutely no one . . . can really
ever replace a truly-great mother. to me, she was my ideal.

where once she had mixed up homemade cakes with great
frostings before bedtime, she now could not remember
how. though she lived for years to go shopping, and knew
all the latest styles and fashions, now she could never be
left alone at all. her world had to be very structured, and
kept relatively small.

at the nursing home, people do not think she is an occu-
pant, but a visitor. still with much black in her thick, coarse
hair, jan keeps her looking perfectly wonderful. though she
is thinner than ever (i grew up in a family that NEVER
talked about diets, and did not need to), she is still extremely witty and terrific at the piano.

jan went through so much with my mother before we finally admitted her to the finest nursing home we could
find. my father had eleven little accounts all over the country where he stored away savings for my mother from his
pastoral salaries. it was not much, but it so helped us before we had to surrender her to the nursing home.

every afternoon, jan would come in from her counseling office or picking up the children at school, and find my
mother in a new fix.

"mother, where did you get all those bruises on your legs?" she would ask, shocked.

"why, do i have bruises? i think those are just my varicose veins," my mother would respond casually.

"mommy, you have NEVER had varicose veins like that," jan would say.

"well . . . i do not know. i do not remember falling," said my mother, her large brown eyes inquisitive.

the next afternoon, jan would walk in from the grocery store. there was my mother, walking around the house with her middle finger on her right hand in a cup of hot salt water.

"mommy!" jan would exclaim. "what is wrong with your finger?"

"oh, nothing really. just a little hangnail," nodded my mother.

"let me see, mommy," commanded jan.

out came a swollen finger, completely green.

"mother! your finger!" jan shuddered, in shock.

in the hospital emergency room the doctor said, "how long has your finger been this way, mrs. kiemel?"

"why, i do not know. just a few hours," shrugged my mother, casually.

jan shook her head in weak dismay. she had not remembered my mother's finger being *green*.

taking a small knife, the doctor lanced it, and my mother never made a sound. jan nearly fainted. by the time the nurse wrapped her finger, it was such a huge stick of white gauze that she could not use the hand at all. that was the start of jan pulling on her panty hose for her . . . hooking her bra . . . washing her false teeth. (fortunately, i was blessed with teeth like my father. never a cavity, or plaque either. my mother claims it is because she ate multiple oranges, every day, through her pregnancy with jan and me.)

almost every night, my mother would end up in bed with tom and jan. she slept down the hall with little christian, my nephew who is taylor's age. at some point in the night, she would awaken. lose her way down the hall. stumble in the master bedroom, and tom or jan would awaken with her beside them.

one night, jan went into christian's room to kiss him and my mother goodnight.

"we have a strange man visiting in the house," commented my mother.

"we do?" exclaimed jan. "where, mother?"

"down in that other bedroom. tom-something. do you remember his name?" asked my mother quizzically.

"mother? that is tom, MY HUSBAND! remember, mommy?"

"oh," she shook her head, with a distinct look on her face.

one night, jan jumped out of bed, terrified by a loud crash. stumbling, through the dark, to christian's room, she found my mother standing, swinging her arms around.

"mommy! what are you doing? it is three o'clock in the morning?" asked jan.

"exercising," replied my mother with enthusiasm.

she hid her purse all over the house, sure people were trying to take her money. then she would forget where she hid it. she and jan would look for hours for it.

"those little boys around here," she would say, "that tall, red-cheeked one and the other two . . . they keep trying to steal all my money," mother would hound jan.

to really have known my mother in college . . . in her prime . . . the ninetieth percentile clear across her college boards . . . playing the piano for thousands at thirteen . . . reupholstering furniture and making us little dresses after designer clothes at the store. to really have known and enjoyed the beautiful and classy ruth geraldine nash kiemel only then could you understand the pain and sadness we have felt, watching this happen.

we have had to learn to laugh in order to survive. not to waste into some deep depression. within a six weeks' period, i felt orphaned . . . motherless and fatherless. a year later, i still have waves of sadness and deep loneliness wash over me.

i am a lot like my mother. i want everything in order. neat. clean. immaculate.

"jan, honey, you need to clean off the top of your refrigerator," commented my mother, over and over. so like me, but jan would laugh.

"mother, you and ann are two of a kind. just sit on the other side of the table and you will not notice it."

the lovely little lady that shares a room with my mother in the nursing home now is a retired nurse, who for years supervised an entire hospital. she is *perfect* for my mother. adores my mom. looks after her. never married. forgotten most everything, too. she is as convinced as my mother that someone has taken all her money.

we *never* call it a "nursing home," only the "retirement center." several times, my mother has gotten out of bed in the night and fallen. one time, she broke her hip and had hip surgery. at seventy-seven, my mother entered the hospital for the first time since she delivered us.

once, she looked at jan and said, "honey, let's get out of this hotel. it is third rate. we want something with a double bed in it!"

now they tie my lovely mother into position at night. straps everywhere. they find her, over and over, sitting in her chair, having figured someway to untangle herself. they call her the "modern houdini."

recently, jan bought her a pair of white tennis shoes because everyone wore them in the nursing home, and they gave her support. i was visiting from idaho.

"how do you like my new shoes?" asked my mother. "they are the latest thing. everyone is wearing them."

crawling into bed beside her, i laughed and laughed. kissed and kissed her. held her hand. God is so good to me. it means so much to have my mother. she really is fun, and oh so very sweet. alzheimer's can be something rather peaceful for a happy-natured person like my mom. if i can be that fun and sweet at her age, then i will trust Jesus with that. it is not something i fear terribly. yet, if i forget ANYTHING, i become shaken with fear. maybe i am one of the youngest to develop alzheimer's? how easily one develops that thought when you watch someone as sharp as your mother with it.

jan and i were harmonizing old hymns for my mother in the beautiful lobby area of the home. a little lady, in a wheelchair next to us, began clapping her hands in rhythm with our songs.

"she is a little lame up here," smiled my mother, pointing to her brain.

never before have i truly loved and appreciated people in nursing homes. i was often horrified by the thought of them. now, as i visit my mother, with jan, i feel great love for each one. the petite, white-haired lady banging the tray on her wheelchair with a spoon. another who grabs my hand, and asks if i have seen her student? the little boy she is teaching all the prepositions to?

"ann and jan, go introduce yourselves to all my neighbors," my mother pleads each time. "tell them you are my twin daughters."

she is still instinctively a mother. showing off her children. exposing some of her worth.

"jan, your skirt is a little short, honey. no one here ever wears them that length anymore," nods my mother in disapproval.

"i know, mommy," smiles jan. "this is a retirement center. remember?"

a beautiful nurse's aide, mother of seven, cares for my mother. knows Jesus, too. goes in on her days off to wash and fix my mother's hair. to say our names over and over so she will not forget us. Jesus put her in that nursing home, assigned to my mother. He did that because when i was a child, she fed other mother's sons who were in the service, and far from home. she loved so many other mothers and women. now God has put someone there . . . pam . . . to love her.

‚ ‚ ‚

my mom's sister (my great aunt betty knight—twelve years younger than my mom) wrote:

It was in the height of the depression, the year 1927, I arrived in the house of parents nearly forty years of age. Two older children, thirteen and eleven, completed the family.

My father, a happy-go-lucky Scotch Irish businessman was the perfect example of grace—then my mother represented the fiery, disciplined teacher of the law—teaching us biblical literature for twenty minutes every morning.

But my sister, Ruth, loved me also—loved me as I was and taught me of the world. Lugging me around everywhere she went, I discovered my first sense of aroma. It was at the corner drugstore—the smell of ice cream. Ruth had a sweet tooth and taught me the science of savoring a chocolate soda. Beginning with the cherry on top while letting the ice cream slowly, very slowly dissolves into the burning cold soda, that rich creamy liquid, which must be sipped leisurely as the ice cream is eaten with a tall spoon at a faster pace. Our drugstore visits were never rushed but I learned to savor the moments of smell and taste.

She taught me style—my self image made visible—making my dresses—originals designed just for me—then gathering up a ponytail from my thick blonde buster brown straight hair, she topped off my left side always with a large taffeta bow. "God was truly in His heaven and all was right with the world," in those days.

Mother prayed that this child would possess a gift to give back to God and His church. Ruth had the gift of learning and playing the piano—everything from hymns to Gershwin and Cole Porter. She was a natural accompanist, adapting to each style. She was playing for camp meetings so popular in that era beginning in her teens and shared this talent all through her life.

We never knew who was going to appear around our table— whether a debate team coached by Gertrude Taylor—as we lived near a college, or ministers, missionaries or everyday people from our little mission church. But Ruth enjoyed design and setting a mood—she always wanted the house to look just a little "lived in"—kind of a studio effect I call it. Of course there wasn't any money and her delight was to see what she could concoct with combinations of new inexpensive slip covers for the couch and a vase of white spirea that grew in banks around our house, and perhaps changing the furniture around a bit.

We learned in those days and she still believes this and so do I, that it's more fun to create than to go out and buy everything.

So with the calm of our father and the will of my mother, Ruth became the creative wine poured out in her whole life in ministry.

Someone once said "if you have class you don't need much of anything else."

What is class?

Class never runs scared. It is sure-footed and confident in the knowledge that you can meet life head-on and handle whatever comes along.

Jacob had it. Esau didn't. Symbolically, we can look to Jacob's wrestling match with the angel. Those who have class have wrestled with their own personal angel and won a victory that marks them thereafter.

Class never makes excuses. It takes its lumps and learns from past mistakes.

Class is considerate of others. It knows that good manners are nothing more than a series of small sacrifices.

Class bespeaks an aristocracy that has nothing to do with ancestors of money. The most affluent blueblood can be totally without class while the descendant of a Welsh miner may ooze class from every pore.

Class never tries to build itself up by tearing others down. Class is already up and need not strive to look better by making others look worse.

Class can "walk with kings and keep its virtue and talk with crowds and keep the common touch." Everyone is comfortable with the person who has class because he is comfortable with himself.

If you have class you don't need much of anything else. If you don't have it, no matter what else you have, it doesn't make much difference.

ta ta ta

when Jesus is your First Love, you remember that He is going to do what He needs to do to get us ready for Heaven. He is no respecter of persons. we cannot possibly figure out what specific things He will allow in our lives. ultimately, it doesn't matter how He preps us for the Celestial City. only that we are His. that we have given our best while we could. we must not hold tightly to pride, for life will humble each of us in God's own creative way.

many times, i have watched people become more overtly what they really are, inside, in old age, either sweet and gentle and warm . . . or cranky and nasty and mean.

"Jesus, cleanse my life, utterly. please make me more and more like You! whether i am mentally alert, or not . . . physically impaired, or strong . . . may my face shine and my eyes sparkle with Your grace."

soon after will and i married, we visited corrie ten boom. crippled into almost a fetal position from multiple strokes . . . unable to do ANYTHING for herself . . . yet with brilliant, intense, bright blue eyes . . . she was utterly transparent with Divine love and warmth. she prayed for will and me in her native tongue. she was still allowing her First Love to affect lives.

To be like Jesus—
to be like Jesus—

all through life's journey
to be like Him . . .
from earth to Heaven . . .
to be like Him!

Oh, to be like Thee—
oh, to be like Thee—
Blessed Redeemer, pure as Thou art—
come in Thy sweetness—
come in Thy fullness—
stamp Thine own image, deep on my heart.

        (Thomas O. Chisholm and
          William J. Kirkpatrick)

17. mommy, will you walk me to the school door?

it was friday. my one day at the office each week. getting four small children up. bathed. dressed. matching socks and shoes. teeth brushed (after fixing breakfast). hair combed. faces clean. a list laid out for my WONDERFUL cleaning lady, kay, who has come every friday for nine years.

i had to look professional. collect my briefcase and odds and ends to pack to the office. fix my hair. make-up. toss clothes in the laundry room. then pile four children, packed with energy and distractions, into seat belts. this may not sound too difficult, but i felt i had lived a whole day out by 9 a.m.!

tiffany was driving us. taylor was between us in the front seat. the other three in back. will had long ago left for his office. my lap was piled with books, papers, briefcase, and the diaper bag.

we were barely going to be on time. brock's and taylor's kindergarten and first grade teachers are saints. living right by the angels. fran and dixie and jodie smile sweetly, as my children come either too early or too late almost every day. i pray every day for Jesus to help me with this! both their schools are private, Christian schools. across town. taylor starts at 8:15 a.m. brock goes at 12:15 p.m. they both are done at 3 p.m. between all of those drives, i try to focus on the babies. the house.

that friday it was frigid. drizzling rain. swift wind.

"taylor, today you can walk to the school door alone. you are a very big boy. six years old. strong and self-reliant. honey, mommy's lap is piled with stuff. it is raining. the little ones have to be dropped at the babysitter's. you can do it!"

with great affirmation, i challenged taylor. he and brock always want me to hop out of the car and walk them in to their classrooms. i love doing it. there are some mornings i have only a coat thrown over my nightgown. no make-up. it is very humbling!

"no, mommy," taylor sighed. "please—"

"darling, i cannot do it today! you jump out and i will watch you until you are inside," i persisted.

he quietly crawled out, lunch box in one hand, dragging his back pack in the other hand. slowly, he walked to the school door while many children came dashing in, yelling,

"hi, taylor!"

"i like your sweater, taylor!"

suddenly, while i was turned around quieting the babies, i felt the door open. taylor crawled over me, fighting tears as fiercely as he could

"taylor, darling, what is wrong?" i exclaimed.

"mommy, please . . . "

my blue-eyed, freckled, handsome six year old, looked at me. straight "A" student. advanced reader. sweet disposition.

i dissolved! tossing everything off my lap, into the seat, i fought the wind tearing through my sweater and hair, clinging to his small, soft hand. when we walked in, his teacher was in the hall.

"taylor, what is wrong, honey?" she asked. "i love you. you can tell me."

he lowered his head, embarrassing tears running through his light freckles. taylor does not like to cry in front of any-one though we encourage all our boys to cry when they need to.

"can i see him around the corner?" i asked.

pulling my child to a private spot, i got on my knees and wrapped him in my arms. i began to sob.

"oh, taylor, i love you so much! i love you more than life. more than air to breathe. honey, i did not know it meant that much to you. mommy is so honored that you are proud of me, that we are such great buddies. i will never again not walk you in when you ask me."

wrapping taylor close to me, we both cried silently. then he stood up, wiping the tears off his face.

"mommy, are the tears gone?

does it look like i have been crying?"

"honey, no one will notice."

he hugged my neck. kissed me.

"mom, i will see you this afternoon. okay?"

"yes, taylor. i will be here at three o'clock."

i cried all the way to my office. my children are young
such a short time. soon they probably will not even want
me to show my face around school. they will be so indepen-
dent and self-directed.

a small gesture. a brief moment. every day, i treasure those
walks with taylor and brock. laughing. happy. together. a
treasure. one of my favorite experiences continues to be the
feel of my little sons' hands wrapped in mine.

over and over, i squeeze a hand three times. "i love you."

my child knows to squeeze back twice. "how much?"

then i tug on it as tightly as i can. then he does the three
squeezes first. and laughs as i make faces, pretending he is
breaking my bones.

can i walk with you a mile? or even twenty? or clear to the
end of the journey? i really would like to. it would just feel
good knowing we are traveling together through the good
times and the hard ones.

at taylor's graduation from kindergarten, his teacher, fran
wadsworth, wrote this poem—

Taylor was late every once in a while.
But he came in with no fear just a big smile.
He's really an exceptionally bright little lad
who picked my school, boy, am I glad!!
He has a kind, pleasant personality.
Will bring lots of joy to his parents, friends
    and family.
Taylor away you now must go.
But, Brock will come next—another bright one,
    I know.

18. mommy, tell me
that story again

brandt and colson were snuggled in their cribs, asleep after a long day of being home with me. i would love to have a full-time cook and housekeeper and errand girl besides. someone to do the laundry, and put it all away. then i could spend hours reading books to my sons. baking cookies with them. watching them sleep. anyway . . .

taylor and brock curled up in the big waterbed in the master bedroom, with me. will is great about putting them to bed. telling them continuing sagas of "coco and bobo." i usually try to spend time with them after dinner, too.

we had read a couple of books together. my arm around each child. cozy. warm. fun.

"taylor and brock, would you like me to tell you more about when you were born?"

"yes . . . yes!"

"well . . . mommy and daddy love each other very much. we so wanted to be a family with children. daddy always wanted lots of children, and so did i . . ."

"mommy . . . God gave you two brown-eyed boys and two blue-eyed boys." brock inserted, eyes sparkling. he is AL-WAYS thinking.

"yes, darling, God did. anyway, every time a baby started growing in mommy's tummy, God decided that baby should be in heaven with Him. i cried and cried. we prayed and prayed.

"one day, a special girl called and said she was pregnant. she was expecting a baby. the Lord whispered to her that she was carrying this baby for us. we were so excited!

"we bought that pretty, white crib. i picked out my favorite baby things at stores. soon, this beautiful girl arrived in idaho. daddy and i were there at the hospital when she de-livered you, taylor."

"mommy . . . mommy," taylor tugged on my arm. "was i real tiny? did i have little fingers and toes?"

"oh, taylor, we rushed to the nursery. moments after you were born. daddy thought all the other babies, except you were common . . . but you were BEAUTIFUL!"

taylor and brock, stretched across my lap and legs, totally spellbound. faces glistening.

"taylor, i bent down and spoke your name, and you jerked your little head toward me, and opened your eyes. you knew my voice! i will never forget it. we thought the whole world was celebrating with us!"

"mommy, what do we call that?" brock asked.

"adoption. it means you are extra special. you are chosen specially. you are extraordinary, and not ordinary. God has special plans for you. let me tell you about brock."

his huge, brown eyes twinkled.

"brock, you were just as special a gift. after taylor came, we wanted him to have a brother or sister to play with. again, we prayed and prayed. mommy learned she was pregnant several times, and i lost the babies again.

"out of the blue, a letter came from another very special girl. she told us that a friend had loaned her one of my books to read. that she was expecting a baby. that she thought it was our baby."

"mom, was she pretty like susan and sarah?" taylor asked, full of smiles.

taylor and brock loved colson's and brandt's birthmothers when they flew in to deliver. it seemed so understandable to them. so normal.

"yes, taylor, both of the birthmothers that carried you and brock are beautiful girls. it takes so much love to carry a baby for someone else."

"brock, daddy and i were right there when you popped your head out. i started crying because you were so beautiful, and the doctor handed you right to me. you had lots of black, curly hair. you were our biggest baby! nine pounds, two ounces!"

looking into the faces of my two oldest sons, my eyes moistened. the love i felt for them, and their birthmothers, was

completely impossible to describe. the memories of their
births . . . of an eleven month old and a newborn after so
much anguish and loss. the bedroom was suddenly filled
with a feeling of wonder. stars and hearts and balloons . . .
and two little boys lost in the wonder of it all with me.

"mom!" brock sat up. "mom, you said we were extraordinary. well, is jennifer ordinary or extraordinary? and how
about jessica and jake?"

i should have known brock would come up with such a
question. jennifer and jessica and jake were some of our
FAVORITE kids, but they were not adopted. i could hear
brock telling them that his mommy said they were
"ordinary"!

"mommy," taylor crawled up close to my face. "tell us that
whole story again. please! right now."

"yes, mommy," pleaded brock. "i love that story."

"so we grew in somebody's tummy, too, mommy?" asked
taylor.

"yes, and daddy and i will ALWAYS be so grateful. God
has the BEST ideas. if you had become our children any
other way, it would not have been nearly so special. we
would never have had four little boys as special. you both
and colson and brandt."

this is our story. for us, it is sacred. i pray our children will
never tire of hearing it. will never lose sight of its truly miraculous content. i will tell all of them, over and over, how
God created them for us.

19. a live-in cook for six weeks

a silver-haired, beautiful woman around sixty worked and cooked for my dear friends, the wylies, in cedar hill, texas. one summer, when taylor and brock were small, i went for a visit and fell in love with helen. she made fabulous biscuits and fried chicken and gravy. great pies.

after some time, she moved to another part of texas, and i began to pray. it had been so hard for me to recover my strength, from the hysterectomy . . . my dad's death . . . and other events. i would look in magazines like *good housekeeping*, and stare in awe at these gorgeous layouts of food and feasts. beautiful tables. children elegantly dressed. women with flair, perfect skin and hair.

how do these women put it all together? really? i barely get the kitchen cleaned up before it is time for lunch. i am exhausted by dinner, and getting hamburgers on the table. with four hungry mouths, water being knocked over . . . well, *good housekeeping* is bigger than life to me!

if i had helen, we could seem so perfect. wonderful smells, constantly from the kitchen. hot bread out of the oven. so much time for me to enjoy the children. great nourishment and little effort on my part.

again, i was truly convinced that my stress . . . my weakness . . . my frayed nerves at times . . . were all a result of outward circumstances. would not ANY woman with all the pieces i had be stressed? i kept looking for relief, instead of cure . . . and relief surely worked for awhile.

everything about helen was positive. fine, solid believer. immaculate with herself and the house. her husband and only son had both died, and i have never known ANYONE, before or since, who trusted God so completely. who truly believed in God's way.

she was self-contained. private. very even. not temperamental.

the Lord had put on helen's heart a deep desire to come help me. whatever i wanted to pay. will was again willing to trust me, and what i felt i needed.

"mommy, can miss helen bake cookies with us . . . like you?" clapped taylor.

"oh, yes, taylor, she can help you cook all kinds of wonderful things. besides, mommy will have much more time to spend, focused on you."

"does she make pancakes?" brock called.

we were all excited. it really seemed like the miracle answer for our lives.

miss helen flew in, and she did everything we had hoped. never had we eaten such dreamy, yummy, tasty things. never had we felt more loved and special. it was a tremendous relief to have her—and i believe my health did take a dramatic change for the better.

"miss helen," called taylor, "look at what brandt is doing."

"miss helen, how old are you?" asked brock.

"do you think we could have waffles this morning, miss helen?" i would chirp.

it was hard for me to fathom that some women lived with live-in cooks for years!

one evening, during the Easter season, helen was sitting on the floor in our television room, watching the film "Jesus" on channel six. i was doing some laundry. taylor, brock, colson and brandt were playing with their police cars and helicopters.

walking by the t.v. room to carry folded laundry upstairs, i noticed that two-year-old colson had gone back in and sat down beside her on the floor. for forty-five minutes, colson did not breathe a word or sound. he sat very close to miss helen, the cherubic face raised in total concentration on the resurrection of Jesus.

that colson would leave the exciting play with the other boys . . . that, at two, he would quietly crawl over right next to miss helen, beautiful, small face upturned. not a noise for close to an hour. amazing.

needless to say, miss helen just had a special love for colson. he, from that time on, was the little king in her eyes. i think he got by with more than any of the others. however, no one seemed to care. the other boys laughed over colson's antics and seemed to celebrate him as much as miss helen.

after six weeks, it was time for miss helen to return to texas. it was time for me to take over the house. to roll up my sleeves and be the normal cook, dishwasher, floormopper, clothesfolder.

we will always love miss helen, and feel she is a part of our family. we will think of her especially when we eat twice-baked potatoes or hot biscuits or fresh, chicken-pot-pie.

for six weeks i felt like a queen. i rode bikes almost every day with the children. my hours carried great value and focused attention with my family.

i did feel much better. my enthusiasm mounted. yet, shortly after miss helen left, i found myself slipping back into the abyss of great fear. of old habit patterns that had still not changed. patterns that did not reveal a genuinely cleansed, restored, spirit-filled adventure!

though we would NEVER trade the experience with miss helen, i am reminded again that external forces . . . external blessings . . . exhilarating and unforgettable, do not cleanse one's heart. or purify our pain. they give quick relief, and during that time, i was too weak and beat up to genuinely go after cure.

Jesus takes each of us down our own paths. He allows us to help Him along the way. ultimately, however, He steps in and calls us to accountability.

seeking and finding cures for life's issues involves complex, heart-wrenching choices directed to refine us and purify us. in time we find ourselves genuinely experiencing wellness.

if you live in a crowded, small apartment . . . if your salary is very meager . . . if your children wear only second-hand clothes . . . it cannot damper your joy. crowd out your peace. if we are filled with God's Spirit, we can be content no matter what. will you be patient while i keep learning that, too?

20. anna grows up

when i lived in boston, my focus was different places. everyone i encountered. business men. young women and wives. the tailor. the travel agent. neighbors on the waterfront. most of all, though, children. giving to those early children prepared me for many joys with my own.

taking treats, i would hop a cab to different areas of boston, and deliver the candies to all the children. as i have written in the past, i took children with me on trips. twenty-four children and adults to israel to run my first marathon. eight adolescent girls the next year to israel. i, inspired by the Lord, built a gymnasium in the heart of boston's north end, in the basement of an old building . . . for children in the crowded, asphalt jungle to have room to play.

anna was one of my very, very special little girls. even as i write this, i can see that sweet, pretty face. the dreamy look in her eyes. her thin, small figure blown along by the wind.

alone. standing against the skyline of a powerful city.

anna lived with her mother and sister in a government-subsidized apartment, tiny and crowded. but at least warm, with a roof over their heads.

often, anna would wander into my office at lewis wharf, after her parochial school ended.

"anna, have you had breakfast today?" she would shake
her head "no."

"anna, did you have lunch at school?" again, a
negative nod.

she had a wonderful mom, but it took them bolstering
great courage to survive.

often anna and i would go up to my condominium on the
fourth floor. collect some food items for her to take home
to her mom. other times, i would buy groceries, and put
them in her arms . . . heading home.

one day, i had an idea. "anna, this is OUR secret. just between you and me. okay?" her pretty, pale head nodded af-
firmatively.

"here is some money for you to go shopping with," i
smiled. "a new dress. a skirt. whatever you like!! i must
leave on a speaking trip, but i will send debbie (the gym
director's wife) with you. when i come home, you can sur-
prise me."

giving debbie a hundred dollars (fifteen years ago, that was
a little more valuable), i sent them off to have fun. i
boarded a plane for another direction.

returning home a few days later, i took anna and some others for pizza and ice cream. a little extra treat since i had
been gone a day or two longer. the girls took turns sitting
on my lap. telling me the varying events in their lives. all
of them except anna. she looked beautiful. her eyes shined.
she was radiant. and silent.

outside the little pizza spot, on a corner in the italian north end, each child hugged and kissed me good-bye. anna waited to be last. throwing her arms around me, glistening eyes, she whispered in my ear.

"do you like my jacket? ann, do you like my jeans? i bought them all with your money. things i have always wanted. oh, thank you, ann."

the expression in her voice . . . on her face . . . was unforget-table. holding her in my arms, looking down into this fresh, small face, i began singing to anna. . . .

"freely, freely you have received . . . freely, freely give. go in My Name . . . and because you believe, others will know that I live. . . . "

"anna, you are small. someday, you and a giant God will change the world." i spoke, my heart stirred, alive with deep conviction.

today, anna is in college. getting ready to graduate. a mira-cle. so much courage it took to hold on . . . to give her best. to keep embracing God's dreams.

anna writes me. some of my friends, such as erika and cindy, have truly loved her with me. she came once to idaho, when will and i brought her and some other inner-city kids.

recently,
she wrote the sweetest
poem.

A Name Very Small
My name is Anna,
A name very small
But someday will be bigger than all.

I plan all my goals
Try hard every day,
Those who stop me
All push away.

People should not judge me
For to them I am new,
But soon they will see me
Forever shine through.

How wonderful it will be
When those people finally see
Anna wasn't so small
No, not at all.

Not daffy not dippy
Or others as such.

No! the name is Anna
Said with a delicate touch.

anna, you are a woman now. Jesus has put His hand on
you. stand strong. never hold your heart away from the
Savior's touch. run to win. do not compromise. God's sunrise will cover you. as you read this, remember, i love you
and i care.

21. talking with henry

some great . . . genuinely great . . . people have helped me
in the last couple years. jim and shirley dobson. dr.
archibald hart and his wife, katherine. larry burkett. a one-
night performance by mike warnke. beverly lahaye. loving
notes from chuck colson. henry brandt.

i am very grateful for each influence.

going to jo and henry's (my in-laws) was very strategic in
my journey back to my First Love. for years henry has
helped thousands of couples in their marriages. thousands
of people in their problems.

he went through all the training and educational process of
getting his doctorate in marriage and the family. he ended
up with a brilliant, creative method . . . gently listening
from a biblical perspective.

will and i had been having some struggles. our response to
four babies in three-and-a-half years. some financial rever-
sals. numerous infections. saying nothing of all the surgeries, and their traumas. a major move, and renovation of the
home place.

i had been through some angry stages with will. now, suddenly, i discovered he was more and more angry with me.
we love each other passionately. but there was just a band

of stress and tension that snapped back and forth every
now and then.

for example, will decided we needed structure. this led to
conflict.

growing up, we had a great deal of structure in my home. i
do confess that with four very young children (to say nothing of all the other things in my life), a lot of strict order
was harder for me to maintain than will. i am the softer
touch.

i am wondering if anyone can identify with any of this?
probably these are pretty basic family issues. when you
have two very strong people, each with definite ideas,
there can be clashes.

if a clash occurred, i would say to the little boys, "mommy
loves your daddy so much! you are the luckiest little boys
in the world. will you forgive mommy for getting upset?
will you?"

looking each one in the eye, i would make every child nod
"yes" so i could feel forgiven, and go on.

will worked through his guilt by grabbing me and giving
me a big kiss in front of the little boys, while they giggled.

it is easy, though, to end up like the two of us were in different cars, going the same direction . . . yet we felt less
and less in sync . . . more obvious that we were not a team
. . . we were becoming opponents.

will's anger was more overt. i smiled quietly. shook my
head. did not react much. i did not know it was still down

inside me, all covered with a sweet look and poise. that is, until henry got a hold of me. a hold of will.

helping edit henry's latest book, will's life began to show in the light. as will worked on the spiritual lessons in henry's chapters, he began to see his own sin more and more. where he had always been a purist . . . lived a life of great integrity . . . he failed to see his sinfulness. self-control had completely gotten a hold of him. he saw himself as basically a good person. i saw myself that way, too.

we both felt the title of henry's new book was unusual . . . we identified . . . *When You're Tired of Treating the Symptoms and You're Ready for a Cure, Give Me a Call!* . . . we did.

flying to florida, to my in-laws' condominium hanging over the atlantic ocean . . . the sandy beach literally below us . . . will and i found ourselves seeking henry's help.

marriage and children really bring out what is in one's heart. at least it sure did with us.

i flew into west palm beach feeling very fragile and scared. will's personality was to plunge into this relationship, head first, and fix it. recently, since working with henry's material, i was intrigued by the change i had sensed in will. but i, not wanting henry and will to pin me against the wall, was quiet and distant, trying to protect myself from the blows that i knew must be coming. i really did not think i was angry.

two things i had decided. first, the Lord had basically cleansed me from all my anger (i thought). second, in living with will anderson, i had to be strong and not allow him to crunch me into the ground. seldom did i react to anything. i just did what i wanted to do, on my own. with the house. the children.

this may seem very serious. i think most couples live somewhere in this arena, however. they do rather blend together, and no one notices.

at separate times, in different places, henry spent time with will and then me. he knew just how to handle each of us. for an hour at a time, he would become our counselor. afterwards, so smoothly one could not notice, he put on the hat of father-in-law.

henry seemed to understand will because he was married to will's mother. he also had some feeling for my world. we both function in similar places, writing books and speaking. it was a puzzle magnificently fit together by the Great Designer. the Lord Himself. and Jesus ALWAYS does something . . . anything . . . better.

not being in henry's consultations with will, i focused solely on my own issues as did will. we did not discuss how to create a better marriage. henry tried to listen to things i said that would reveal any problems with some spiritual principle in me.

in the second session, he quietly announced that he perceived i was angry. that, of course, it was between God and me . . . and only God and me. but submerging a lot of the things i really felt was making me sick. the stress of it all buried inside me could kill me. i stumbled off to seek God.

this could not be true . . . that i was angry! i did not feel angry! my defenses were up! slowly, quietly, i began to

pray simply for Jesus to reveal my sins to me. laying my
heart on the floor beside me, utterly exposing it to His
Light, i became more and more shocked.

sins of anger, deceit, contentiousness, rebellion. the Lord
began giving me specific examples in my mind. times with
will. with the children. with others. idolatry. they were
such shocking revelations to me that i began to cry and feel
literally sick. all around me, i felt the forces of God and evil
battling for my soul. it terrified me. it broke me.

remembering a Scripture verse that henry had repeated . . .
that i had learned as a small child . . . helped. "if we confess our sins He is faithful and just to forgive us our sins,
and to cleanse us from all unrighteousness." (1 john 1:9)

confess. with every example God brought to my mind of
any of my sins, i began to confess to Him. to genuinely re-
pent. to ask the Holy Spirit to fill me. i was not sure i even
understood exactly all the pieces of the process. Christ's
love and redemption and the sudden realization of my sinfulness all overwhelmed me.

> There is not night but in His light
> you will never walk alone . . . always feel at home
> . . . wherever you may roam.
> there is no power can conquer you
> if God is on your side.
> Do not be discouraged . . .
> just go to Him and hide . . .
>
> It is no secret what God can do.
> What He has done for others,
>   He will do for you.
> With arms wide open,

He will pardon you.
It is no secret what God can do.

(Stuart Hamblen)

yes, i had received Jesus when i was eight years old at a
billy graham movie. yes, i had committed my entire life to
Jesus as a junior in college. though i had fallen on my face
now and then, i had NEVER reverted from that commitment. I was totally sincere.

this experience was different. it was like believing i was on
this straight path, heading down the road toward heaven.
without even knowing it, the subtleness of sin had pulled
me astray, weaving me farther and farther away. off
course. i just had not realized it. the world had blinded my
sight. my heart. softened my true level of honesty. diluted
my depth, my commitment to Jesus.

though i thought everything was okay with me . . . that outside forces like being a public person, a mother of four toddlers, a wife to such a strong personality as will's . . . had
created my stress and physical breakdown . . . i was wrong.

"keep your heart with all diligence for out of it come the issues of life." (proverbs 4:23)

my heart . . . my peace . . . my joy . . . my health are not dependent on outside forces and people. my serenity and
love are utterly and completely dependent on the condition
of my heart. to see how truly dirty and over-stuffed-with-
sin my heart had truly gotten . . . made me want to wretch.
as i am trying to articulate this, it is very painful and hard.

will found me crying. jo and henry had gone for several hours to do errands. without knowing the pain and wreckage in me, he took my hand, and had to nearly force me down to the ocean for a long walk on the sand. fast. brisk wind in my face. taste of salt on my tongue. inside my heart was a caldron of raging pain and grief.

at moments i wanted to get on the next plane and go home to my babies . . . to run from what i was seeing . . . then i became angry with will and then henry for causing me pain . . . then i had to confess . . . henry was right.

was there anything else i should do? was i even worthy enough to live? oh, if there was only some kind of penance. some kind of emotional release.

what happened was that things quietly began to change. my physical pain started easing. i became less and less afraid of pain. my muscles began to relax. i felt clean and free and released inside. i saw will in a different light. the Holy Spirit was right there for me to call on. instantly. He was my Source of peace. He really was. outside forces could not seem to shake me.

i did not become perfect. never will i be there. but i am back on the straight road.

will and i realized how easy it had become to lose our friendship. we were strangers when we married, really . . . i think most people are . . . and we never figured out how to truly play on the same team. we had both been bosses. in charge of our own lives. we tended to compete on all fronts, rather than blend.

Jesus did something in us. we started over. we let go of
what was behind us. we really, truly became friends. not in
our own power. or our own strength. but being deeply broken by our individual sinfulness. repenting. and renewing
hearts.

᷂   ᷂   ᷂

today, as every day, holds a fresh call to confession and re-
pentance. a plea for cleansing. for more of God's spirit.

every day, we will have to work on putting our First Love in
top priority. opening our humanity to all of God's grace. then
on each other. another great adventure. we count few things,
today, of much importance . . . beyond this and our children.

we commit, with conviction, that the world cannot steal
those key loves away. not if our hearts are truly focused on
the One who made us a team and a family.

later and . . . now . . . i ask, "it is so simple. how could i
have missed this? it is just so simple!"

these quotations hold special meaning for me—

> I would have you learn when temptations assail you, and
> the 'enemy comes in like a flood' that this thing is from
> Me, that your weakness needs My might, and your safety
> lies in letting Me fight for you.
>
> (Paul Billheimer)

> Lord, I give up my own plans
>   and purposes, all my own
> desires and hopes, and accept thy

will for my life. I give up myself,
my time, my all, utterly to Thee to be
    Thine forever. Fill me and seal me with
Thy Holy Spirit. Use me as Thou wilt.
    Send me where Thou wilt. Work out
Thy whole will in my life at my
    cost, now and forever.

(Betty Scott Stam)

Hast thou no scar?
No hidden scar on foot, or side, or hand?
I hear thee sung as mighty in the land,
I hear them hail thou bright ascendant star.
Hast thou no scar?
Hast thou no wound?
Yet, I was wounded by the archers spent,
lean me against a tree to die.
Hast thou no wound?

No wound? No scar?
Yet, as the Master shall the servant be
and pierced are the feet that follow Me,
but thine are whole.
Can he have followed far
who has no wound nor scar?

(Amy Carmichael)

Suffering crystallizes a soul's intrinsic
strength; for it is through suffering that a man
of mettle can come into his own,
and fathom his own depths.

It was through suffering that I discovered
how I was, by nature, inclined
to do good. . . .

That without love, I could not work at all.
Time ceased to exist once my
heart was taken over by the
Lord of creation.

(Anwar Sadat, in a special *Time* report about the time
he spent in confinement as a political prisoner)

22. *be prepared for the wilderness*

will and i attend Christ community church in idaho falls where we live. it was the church will had attended when we married, and the one he had truly become a part of. though i had been raised in the nazarene church, and there is a vibrant, growing one in town (with a pastor we love!), i felt i should go where will had established his worship home.

george marriott and richard spencer pastored well the first eight years we were married, but now the church had been in much prayer and searching for God's perfect man for the hour. for a year-and-a-half, will headed the search committee. he sought out the advice of spiritual giants for their help and direction.

"listen, ann, God can do ANYTHING. i have lived in this area for years, and have faithfully prayed for a genuinely great and productive Christian church. there is so much potential in our area. God could pick ANYONE . . . one of the 'greats' . . . to help us change our world," will would challenge me and the church over and over.

many months, i felt discouraged. before marrying, i had made eighteen to twenty appearances a month. most sundays, i was in flight home from another appearance. for

years, i had not been able to really participate in a growing, dynamic church.

when one speaks to large audiences as often as i have and
do, there is a special urgency and need to be ministered to.
to have something enlightening and convicting to be put
back into your life, after so much has been given out.

about five months ago, God sent us our man. the one we
had prayed for so long and earnestly. just as many of us
were about to wonder if God really cared. our fellowship
had grown considerably through Christ's Spirit in richard
spencer. now dave gibson, richard's brother-in-law (both
married to sisters), missionary and professor in a Bible
school in alaska has arrived with his wife, kathy, and their
three children.

again, needs are so important. if needs are met too quickly
. . . before one hardly has a chance to feel the tug and longing for the needs to be met, then one's appreciation is
rather superficial, and gratitude really short-lived.

our pastor and family are genuine and very down-to-earth.
dave is working on his doctorate. kathy homeschools the
children. amy, the fourteen-year-old daughter, is especially
dear to me because i was a preacher's kid, too. i understand the blessings . . . and the real sacrifices . . . of being a
pastor's child.

recently, i packed up some clothes of mine that i thought
were blousey enough to fit her. every time i see amy in a
sweater or skirt i gave her, my eyes moisten with such
love. i want her to grow up, knowing she is special. a girl
with a unique destiny. to know that God is calling her dad
into the ministry is such a blessing and not a curse.

dave is incredibly articulate. a pulpiteer that i feel could compete with anyone.

last week, he preached a sermon on the wilderness of Christian journeys.

holding on to one's First Love . . . demands wilderness experiences to center us.

to lead us toward more wholeness. to purify us with fire. to polish and smooth all our rough edges . . . our sinful corners . . . with His heat of love and conviction. drawing us over and over, back to our First Love.

dave's message on the wilderness, and our deep need to have the perfect companion on the journey, was so poignant that i asked him if i could share some of his thoughts with you.

Jesus Christ Is a Tireless Wilderness Victor And a Perfect Wilderness Companion

Have you ever been into a real wilderness? I don't mean a "tourist trap wilderness" in which you drive your car through some game ranch and look at sleeping animals while you eat chips and sip pepsi in your air conditioned car. I mean a real wilderness. A huge, lonely expanse in which you are faced with beauty and danger, loneliness and splendor, uncertainty and low resources?

In the past several years I have gone into the wilderness on seven or eight different times for three to five days each time. This was real wilderness in which the plane dropped you off and you would not see the plane again for several days. It was forty or fifty miles to the nearest highway and in the distance you would have to cross two rivers and walk on so much wet, spongy muskeg that your legs would never hold out. Rain storms were a certainty, snow storms were a probability, and bear attacks were a possibility.

In those trips I always had another person with me—a wilderness companion—someone to help me if I got into trouble and someone to encourage me in the struggles of wilderness living.

Some of my wilderness companions were not as good as others. Some of them had never been in the wilderness or had a heart attack three years earlier or didn't keep dry and they got sick or did not know what to do in the wilderness or were stoics who did not want to talk.

I have also had some good wilderness companions who have helped me tremendously. I want you to think about the qualities of a good wilderness companion with me. But first I would like to think about the nature of the wilderness itself. When you understand the nature of the wilderness you can understand why wilderness companions are so crucial.

What Is the Nature of the Wilderness?

Jesus was in the Judean wilderness which is a very rugged, very dry, and very barren place. It is rock and sand and mountains and ravines and almost no vegetation. It is a wilderness which has the characteristics of every physical wilderness and every spiritual wilderness and every emotional wilderness.

The wilderness is a place of loneliness. When you are in the wilderness you are terribly lonely. It is quiet and huge and you are desperately alone. In the wilderness you long for someone to talk to. You want so badly for someone to understand, someone to listen quietly and to care. You long for a person who will just care a little about the battles in your life. You want so desperately to pour out your heart to someone. You want to cry and to sob and to unload your whole burden. But no one is there. No one cares. No one listens. NO one turns aside from their own pursuits for just five minutes to give you a listening ear and a caring word. The open wound of pain is compounded by the salt of loneliness. It is bad enough to be hurt but it is even worse to hurt alone.

When people are alone in the wilderness they feel so lonely they begin to talk to themselves. I have done it. I have spent a long time just singing to hear the sound of my own voice.

A wilderness is a lonely place—without a companion, you will talk to yourself.

The wilderness is a place of fear and danger. The wilderness is also a place of fear. You can be afraid of an attack there. You can be afraid of being lost there. You can be afraid of what is happening to those you love while you are in the wilderness. You can be afraid of injury.

Jesus spent forty days in the wilderness in the midst of danger. The text of Mark says that He was "with the wild beasts." What Mark implies is that He was in danger of being attacked by them. This is not a cute, pastoral scene in which Christ is petting lambs and bunnies. This is a threatening "Daniel in the lions' den" scene in which God must protect Him from the lions and bears—both of them existed in the wilderness of Judea.

The wilderness is a place of low resources. The wilderness is a place where you have limited food and water

and clothing and shelter. It is a place where you fear that
you may not have enough to survive. You begin to wonder just how long you can hold out before help comes. In
the wilderness you can run short of emotional resources
or spiritual resources or physical resources or financial resources. In the wilderness you must often ration food and
if help comes too late that may not be enough.

The wilderness is a place of uncertainty. The wilderness
is a place where you don't know for sure what will happen. Will it rain or snow or blow or blizzard? Will the
plane come back in time or will it come back at all? You
begin to spend most of your days watching the southern
horizon—squinting into the clouds and searching for a
small dot. You begin to listen for the whine of that motor.
You hear the whine of the motor in the wind and you create dots in the sky—hoping against hope that help is
coming.

Who knows what will happen in the wilderness—it is a
place of uncertainty.

The wilderness is a place of temptation. The wilderness
is a place of temptation. To the Jews the wilderness was a
place of gloom and the abode of devils and unclean spirits. It is a place where countless Bible characters and
countless modern characters have been enticed to evil.
For example, in the wilderness the Israelites were faced
with low resources and with overwhelming odds. They
were tempted to abandon their trust in God and they
gave in to that temptation by refusing to go into the promised land. Psalm 95 recounts one time when they were
out of water and they succumbed to temptation.

- *David* was forced into the wilderness when his son
  Absalom rebelled. David was in the wilderness running
  for his very life and he was tempted to give up trust
  in God.

- *Jesus* was tested in the wilderness for forty days. Satan spent forty days enticing Him to evil and for forty days He refused evil.

- *American Christians* are habitually tested in the wilderness and the indications are that we are not doing well. Listen to statements of some Christian leaders about American Christianity:

- *John R. Stott:* "American Christianity is 3,000 miles wide and 1/2 inch deep."

- *Pastor Bill Hull:* "Now the difference between Christians and non-Christians has blurred and is fast disappearing. My own experience as a pastor substantiates this belief. Christians' use of money, priorities of time, attitudes about work and leisure, divorce and remarriage, increasingly reflect culture rather than scripture. Therefore, the church is weak in skills and weak in character."

- *Francis Schaeffer:* "Here is the great evangelical disaster—failure of the evangelical world to stand for truth as truth. There is only one word for this—namely accommodation. The evangelical church has accommodated to the world spirit of the age."

- *Pastor Bill Hull:* "We see the church through the narrow lens of success, rather than through the broad lens of holiness and impact."

- *George Gallup:* "Among evangelicals, there are a highly committed group of ten percent. These people carry the load and will make the difference. These 'nonaccommodators' are the 'hell bent for glory group'—(the rest just have fire insurance.)"

- *Dr. Elton Trueblood:* "Perhaps the greatest single weakness of the contemporary Christian church is that millions of supposed members are not really involved at all and, what is worse, do not think it strange that they

are not. As soon as we recognize Christ's intention to
make His church a militant company we understand at
once that the conventional arrangement cannot suffice.
There is no real chance of victory in a campaign if
ninety percent of the soldiers are untrained and unin-
volved, but that is exactly where we stand now. Most
alleged Christians do not now understand that loyalty
to Christ means sharing personally in His ministry.

"Never before has the evangelical faith gotten so
much press and made so little difference. Our numbers
are exploding and our impact is dying."

A major group of American Christians are very nice people. You will not catch them over at the Blue Room on Friday night. But neither will you catch them sharing their
faith, cleaning up their thought life or transferring their
values to their kids. They found themselves in a cultural
wilderness called "pluralistic America" and they gave
up—surrendered to temptation and ease.

The wilderness is a difficult place. It is characterized by
loneliness, fear, danger, low resources, uncertainty and
temptation. It is a difficult place; and therefore it demands a qualified wilderness companion.

What Are The Traits
Of a Good Wilderness Companion?

*A good wilderness companion provides friendship and
communication and understanding.* He is a person who
has been there and can understand and who will be
there. Jesus Christ has stationed Himself at the edge of
every wilderness and goes in with every believer.

• *The three Hebrew children* in the book of Daniel went
  into the fiery furnace and the king saw a fourth Person
  in there. He said, "Look! I see four men loose and walk-

ing about in the midst of the fire; and they are not hurt, and the form of the fourth is like the Son of God" (Daniel 3:25).

- *Stephen* went into the wilderness of martyrdom and as he was about to die he looked up and said, "Behold, I see the heavens opened up and the Son of Man standing at the right hand of God" (Acts 7:46).

- *Paul* went into one spiritual wilderness after another and the Lord said to him, "Do not be afraid but speak and do not keep silent; for I am with you, and no one will attack you to hurt you; for I have many people in this city" (Acts 18:9–10).

Jesus Christ has stationed Himself at the edge of every wilderness and goes in with every believer.

A good wilderness companion is reassuring. He is a person who gives us assurance and courage and hope. He tells us to keep going and not give up. He tells you that He will be there for you. When Jesus Christ left us here He said, "Lo, I am with you always, even to the end of the age" (Matthew 28:20).

A good wilderness companion is a provider. He finds resources for you. He gets you what you need.

Read the gospels sometime and see all the times in which Jesus provided something that someone needed. Jesus Christ is a provider of resources. In fact, one of the key features of eternity when Jesus Christ is ruling completely is that we will never lack anything. We will never be short of money or time or strength or food or anything.

Paul says in Philippians 4:13—I can do all things through Christ who strengthens me.

Jesus Christ is a perfect wilderness Companion because
He is the perfect Provider. In the wilderness everything is
in short supply, but nothing is ever back ordered with
Jesus.

A good wilderness companion is stable. He is a person
who will not panic and run. He is a person who is not up
and down but steady. He is a person who does not com-
plicate bad situations with hysteria.

The Bible continually refers to God the Father and to
Jesus Christ as a "Rock." A rock is stable, it is solid, it
does not move and crumble when the storm hits.

Jesus Christ is a perfect wilderness Companion because
He is a Rock. The storms and quakes of life will move everything except Jesus Christ and those who have built
their houses on Him.

*A good wilderness companion has experience in the wil-
derness.* He has been in there before and he knows what
to do.

Unlike the city slickers who often wander into the wilderness Jesus Christ has been there. He has experience in the
wilderness. Mark says He was in there for forty days.

*A good wilderness companion provides deliverance from
temptation.* A good wilderness companion is someone
who will:

1. Not excuse our sin. They will not dismiss our sin
    and make light of it. They care about us enough to
    hold us accountable.

2. Provide what we need to escape. (see 1 Corinthians
    10:13.)

The key issue for us as Christians is not whether or not we can resist temptation. The key issue is whether we really want to resist temptation. Do I want a Christian faith and a lifestyle that is more than one-half-inch deep? I don't have to succumb to apathy, laziness, filthy thoughts, and bad attitudes because God always provides a way to escape. The problem is in the motivation—it is in the "want to" not in the "how to."

ta ta ta

Every life enters the wilderness from time to time and only Jesus Christ is the perfect wilderness Companion.

Conclusion

Do you know when most wilderness travelers give up hope? It is not when their known resources are gone. Most wilderness travelers give up hope when their companion dies. They may have been in the wilderness with a friend who got lost. They may have been in the wilderness with a person who died or a dog who died or a horse who died. But when their companion dies they are sorely tempted to give up hope.

I want to ask you to remember two things for me:

1. If you have a friend or a family member in a spiritual or emotional wilderness, perhaps their greatest need is for a companion. They need a wilderness companion. You do not have to be a person who fixes everything for them. They do not need a magician who can fix everything. They do not need an anesthesiologist who can numb everything. They do not need a con man who can hide everything. They need a person who is willing to stick with them when they are in the wilderness.

It is often very hard to love people who are in the
wilderness. When they are in a spiritual or emotional or physical or financial wilderness they can
be real unlovable. They can be so preoccupied with
their problems and their own fears that they actually repulse others. People in any wilderness need
you to be their companion.

2. If you go into the wilderness, Jesus goes in with
   you. Jesus Christ has stationed Himself on the edge
   of every wilderness and if you go into any given
   wilderness, Jesus Christ goes in with you. He is the
   perfect wilderness Companion. He provides comfort and empathy in discouragement because He
   has been in there before. He provides accountability
   and deliverance in temptation because He has won
   that battle before. Jesus Christ has stationed Himself
   on the edge of every wilderness and if you go in,
   He goes in with you.

Jesus Christ is a tireless wilderness Victor and a perfect
wilderness Companion.

❧ ❧ ❧

When We See Christ

Often times the day seems long,
our trials hard to bear,
we're tempted to complain,
to murmur and despair:
but Christ will soon appear
to catch His bride away,
all tears forever over
in God's eternal day.

Sometimes the sky looks dark
with not a ray of light,
we're tossed and driven on,
no human help in sight;
but there is One in heaven
who knows our deepest care,
let Jesus solve your problem
just go to Him in prayer.

Chorus:
It will be worth it all
when we see Jesus,
life's trials will seem so small
when we see Christ;
one glimpse of His dear face
all sorrow will erase,
so bravely run the race
'til we see Christ.

(Hymn by Esther Kerr Rusthoi)

23. *sunrise always comes*

if you cling to your First Love—no matter how dark and desolate your path seems—the sunrise will come!

dave and linda were in my book, *Open Adoption.* after eight miscarriages, she had written me a loving letter. sharing their anguish, their childlessness. in the first open adoption outside my own children's, i placed a beautiful, newborn girl in their arms. they named her rebecca ann. she is exceptionally bright and full of spunk.

dave and linda have a hog farm in south dakota. they are some of the most genuine, strong, amazing people i have ever known. for a of couple years, i had been praying for the perfect baby to be a sibling to rebecca . . . and to make them more of a complete family.

a year ago, a lovely, intelligent, older girl, flew in to idaho falls . . . from far away . . . to deliver a baby. she had selected dave and linda as the adoptive couple for her baby. after arriving only three days before delivery, she produced a healthy, darling baby girl.

from the start of this delivery, there were problems. without going into a lot of details, marcy (the birthmother) began to exert her stubborn independence immediately. rather than let dave and linda take the baby from the hospital, as she was released, she took the baby to the home where i was keeping her . . . without telling me or anyone.

marcy's mother flew in for the delivery and was really supportive of the open adoption process . . . and of dave and linda. the baby's father was seemingly unstable. drug problems. fierce temper that led to violence over and over.

marcy confessed, often, to her fear of him. fear for her safety . . . and the baby's. more than anything else, his erratic behavior and the lack of a true relationship with Jesus, were her main motivations to release the baby. to give this baby a real family. a genuine chance.

the birthfather began to fight for custody of the baby. marcy flew to south dakota, with dave and linda, to complete signing of legal documents there. though i had lined up for her to stay just down the road from dave and linda, she talked her way into staying with them. she took control of the baby and more-or-less called the shots.

it became a more and more tense situation. we were all stressed out. waiting for the south dakota judge to sign papers that would allow marcy to go on home, though the birthfather's court battle was still in process.

in defense of marcy, it was very stressful. though i am not sure the waiting around in south dakota had anything to do with it, she used it as a major struggle to letting go.

because i feel fiercely about not letting a girl sense pressure about releasing her baby, i try very hard to make sure it is the girl's decision and no one else's.

at one point, i challenged dave and linda to take the baby to the motel where marcy had gone before her departure.

"dave and linda, are you willing to hand the baby and all her little things back to marcy? to tell marcy to take the baby home? that you really feel she cannot part with her? be sure you tell her that you will always love her, no matter what . . . and that you will pick her and the baby up tomorrow morning for the plane to return home."

they did exactly as i instructed, genuinely sincere. they did not want marcy doing something she was not at peace with . . . and they did not want to become more and more attached to the baby if she was not going to be theirs.

marcy was calling their phone before they even returned home. crying. begging them to take the baby. that it would be a terrible mistake for her to keep her.

days later, marcy, in her home state, testified several days in a row, against the birthfather's character and stability. she said, under oath, that she felt he was unfit to be the father. that she desired dave and linda to be the parents of her child.

there were many pieces to this complicated scenario. each piece threw dave and linda's emotions into chaos. pain. fear. i am sure marcy's life was stretched beyond limits, too.

when the baby was four months old, marcy eloped with the birthfather. absolutely no one knew. they called dave and linda from a distant city, saying they were heading their direction in a car. they would fight for the baby's rights back.

the adoption had cost dave and linda sixteen thousand dollars, with all the legal fees and complicated pieces, (i do

not take money for adoptions), so much more than they
had. they were stretched financially, emotionally, spiritually.

"God, why are You doing this to us?"

how they loved this baby. she was also the answer to
rebecca's prayers, and totally adored by her big sister.

the whole process cost will and me several thousand dollars out of our own pockets. it was especially brutal for me
because i love all sides . . . and i felt so responsible for getting dave and linda into the middle of this.

when one works in adoption, it is important to be prepared
for a kick in the stomach every once in awhile. the enemy
does not like girls being obedient to God's will in their
lives. he does not like infertile couples to find life and sun-
shine and restored hope. though i have ninety–seven percent success in the adoptions i have worked with, most
agency adoptions have only, at the very most, forty percent
success.

when the baby was four months old, dave and linda and rebecca lost her. all their money spent. incredible grief over
losing the baby that had so become a part of them. and it
took courage for me to say i would ever put myself on the
line again.

the past seven-and-a-half months have been very stressful
for this little family. and reasonably so. linda miscarried
her ninth or tenth baby, and their hearts and wills ached
for the priceless little baby they had bonded to. i sent rebecca a doll. something she could bond to. could give her
baby sister's name to. so the loss would not be so great
and acute.

for months, i have searched and prayed for the perfect situation, for this family to adopt another baby. though i work with many girls, i kept waiting for what felt like the right baby for them.

one morning, a few days ago, dave got up very early, and wrote me the following letter. without his knowing that agnes at new hope (my adoption agency) would be calling them later in the day about a baby.

a little boy. just starting his fourth month. (the same age as the baby when they lost her). having to be pulled out of the adoptive home where he had been placed. beautiful, happy child. from pictures, he looked just like dave and linda and rebecca! i stopped in wonder at God's way when i learned that this little boy had been named david before dave and linda came into the picture.

before the miracle . . . before God's plan was revealed . . . dave wrote the following letter of victory.

Dear Ann,

Greetings from South Dakota. I have been wanting to sit down and write you a letter for some time, but have only recently felt the appropriate inspiration to do so. My, how the weeks and months grind by. It was exactly one year ago this very week, that a pregnant woman named Marcy called my wife on the phone for the first time. I must say that now—one year later, life is really starting to feel good again. Linda is doing much better. She has finally finished pulling out the many painful pictures from photo albums. The pain and anger is going away. I sold some hogs last week and a guy is coming for some tomorrow and do you know what? Not one dime of it is going to be sent to a California lawyer.

As a matter of fact, thanks to dear Judge Martin, the birthparents
are reimbursing us for most of our expenses by sending $500.00
a month. At the rate they are going, it will take two years, but
anything is better than nothing. We do not expect or ask for an
expense-free adoption if and when the day comes. All we need is
a little patience and understanding with the finances and all will
be well.

Spiritually, we are doing fine. The situation in the Middle East is
another daily reminder of what or who is truly important in life.
Each day we are reminded of what a special girl Rebecca Ann
is—so strong willed—so full of life and ideas and questions. That
is one area of Linda's and my will that God has broken into little
bitty pieces—the desire to have a brother or sister for Rebecca
Ann. We really do want another baby, but it is not an obsession
or something we "demand that God has to do for us." It is not
an issue of "OK, God, if you really do love me, then do this." It
is more a matter of He knows best. We want His plan first, our
ideas second. For the life of me I cannot imagine the "why" with
the Marcy ordeal. Maybe all God did was use us as cannon fod-
der to spare some other adoptive couple. I don't know. It doesn't
matter anymore.

Well, I best close—enough ramblings. Through it all God has
been merciful to us and I really mean that. There are two things I
would like you to do for us. First—keep praying for us. Second—
encourage the people at Seattle to keep us in mind.

May God bless you as you do a good work.

                                        Dave, Linda,
                                        Rebecca Ann

yes, holding tightly to one's First Love demands wilderness
experiences. exposes our sins and fears for what they really
are. in our pursuit to be holy, and wholly committed to

Jesus, we find ourselves only steps away from one humilia-
tion after another. our hearts and thoughts are searched
and tested and tried. the most private, secretive corners of
our beings are exposed. what is hidden is revealed.

dave and linda lived months, raw with pain and hurt. at
times, fierce anger. tempered by time and God's Holy
Spirit. there were dozens of moments that they really ques-
tioned if God had deserted them. if they even believed in
their First Love.

but they fiercely clung to the slim rays of faith that had created their Christian foundation. when their wills had been
purely tried, and completely crushed, they reached through
the blackest hole, and quietly decided to follow Jesus, no
matter what. in that moment of victory, God began to answer the cry of their hearts.

> Tis true—oh, yes, tis true—
> God's wonderful promise is true—
> for I have tested and proved it and
> tried it—
> and I know God's promise
> is true!
>
> Earthly friends may prove untrue—
> doubts and fears assail—
> but there's One who cares for you
> One who will not fail—
>
> (Lelia N. Morris)

ે ે ે

i see farther down the journey today.
more than ever, "i have set my heart,
like fruit, to do God's will"
Jesus *IS* my First Love
Jesus truly pays!

epilogue:
the Refiner's fire

the recent past . . .
i ran the race with shoes of clay . . .
Jesus loved me with fire . . .
to show me hidden sin . . .
my prayer . . .
be all he knows . . . i can be . . .
running . . . his wings on my shoes . . .
First Love in my heart!

Will Anderson

(this poem captures my heart:)

There burns a fire with sacred heat
white hot with holy flame
and all who dare pass through its blaze
will not emerge the same
some as bronze and some as silver
some as gold, then with great skill
all are hammered by their sufferings
on the anvil of His will

219

chorus:
The Refiner's fire
has now become my soul desire
purged and cleansed and purified
that the Lord be glorified
He is consuming my soul
refining me, making me whole
no matter what I may lose
I choose the Refiner's fire

I'm learning now to trust His touch
to crave the fire's embrace
for though my past with sin was etched
His mercies did erase!
Each time His purging cleanses deeper
I'm not sure I'll survive
yet the strength in growing weaker
keeps my soul alive!*

---

*   words by jon mohr, from the steve green album, *the mission*, 1989. used by permission.

about the author

ann kiemel anderson and her husband, will, live on a forty
acre farm in idaho falls, idaho. ann has written thirteen
books and occasionally speaks around the nation, especially for crisis pregnancy centers and pregnancy hot lines.

she was voted outstanding woman of her graduating class
at northwest nazarene college and was made a member of
phi beta kappa. ann has done some graduate work in jour-
nalism at kansas university and has worked as a public
school teacher at the junior high level in english. she has
also served as a youth director in southern california.

ann enjoys running and has competed in eight marathons.
although she is presently the executive director of an idaho
adoption agency, she spends most of her time as mother to
her four fun-loving sons and as wife to will anderson. will
has sold the potato farm and is currently involved in inter-
national business.

The typeface for the text of this book is *Palatino*. This type—best known as a contemporary *italic* typeface—was a post-World War II design crafted by the talented young German calligrapher Hermann Zapf. For inspiration, Zapf drew upon the writing legacy of a group of Italian Renaissance writing masters, in which the typeface's namesake, Giovanni Battista Palatino, was numbered. Giovanni Palatino's *Libro nuovo d'imparare a scrivera* was published in Rome in 1540 and became one of the most used, wide-ranging writing manuals of the sixteenth century. Zapf was an apt student of the European masters, and contemporary *Palatino* is one of his contributions to modern typography.

Substantive Editing:
Michael S. Hyatt

Copy Editing:
Cynthia Tripp

Cover Design:
Steve Diggs & Friends
Nashville, Tennessee

Page Composition:
Xerox Ventura Publisher
Printware 720 IQ Laser Printer

Printing and Binding:
Maple-Vail Book Manufacturing Group
York, Pennsylvania

Cover Printing:
Strine Printing Company
York, Pennsylvania